BUDGET SAVVY DIVA'S
Guide to Slashing Your Grocery Bill by 50% or More

*Secret Tricks & Clever Tips
for Eating Great & Saving Money*

SARA LUNDBERG

Ulysses Press

Published by
Ulysses Press
P.O. Box 3440
Berkeley, CA 94703
www.ulyssespress.com

ISBN: 978-1-61243-125-3
Library of Congress Catalog Number 2012951886

Printed in the United States by Bang Printing

10 9 8 7 6 5 4 3 2 1

Acquisitions Editor: Kelly Reed
Managing Editor: Claire Chun
Editor: Jessica Benner
Proofreader: Lauren Harrison
Cover design: what!design @ whatweb.com
Interior design and layout: Rebecca Lown
Artwork: BudgetSavvyDiva.com woman logo © BudgetSavvyDiva.com/Kei Phillips,
    shopping cart © Patricia Burke/istockphoto.com

Contents

Introduction

One of my earliest memories is making pizzas on English muffins in the kitchen with my dad. This is just one of many childhood recollections that revolve around cooking with my family.

The importance of a home-cooked dinner—and more important, sitting down to the meal—was instilled in me from a very young age.

My mom showed me how the lemons from the tree in our front yard could be used to keep a chicken moist. Both my parents taught me the importance of having herb and vegetable gardens. I was able to develop not only a green thumb but also how a little rosemary can add something special to a dish.

It was another family member, my grandfather, raised during the Depression, who instilled in me the importance of a dollar. He taught me to think about each purchase I make, because what you need and what you want may be two different things. As I grew, I figured out how to save money while still living a full life—especially in the kitchen. This is the concept that this book is based on: saving money on groceries is easy if you know the right tips and tricks.

The book is full of information that you can use right away! Even if you don't have room to stockpile canned goods or a grocer that does Double Coupon Day, the Budget Savvy Diva is always helping you find ways to save money while still enjoying a luxurious dinner. The keys are learning to think differently about grocery shopping and a few easy, frugal recipes that anyone can make.

CHAPTER ONE

Menu Planning

It's no secret that one of the best ways
to save money (and time!) in the kitchen
is smart menu planning.

Deciding what you feel like eating just before dinner is a luxury that could cost you dearly if you shop at the last minute, or worse, order takeout or head to a restaurant.

Planning for your week's meals allows you to take your inventory—as well as great deals at the supermarket—into account. It even provides a unique opportunity to evaluate your family's daily nutrition and improve your diet.

Proper meal planning saves money by reducing gas mileage with fewer trips to the grocery store, as well as reduced impulse spending when you get there. You also have the opportunity to make meals in bulk, which often means less spent on per-unit costs and more gained in leftovers, aka free meals. Meal planning means you are in control when you shop.

When you buy only what you know you will use, you don't just save money, but time. No more searching your cupboards in a race to mix and match ingredients for some half-baked dinner catastrophe. You can cancel the emergency runs for forgotten items, especially when bulk buying has provided you with a nifty stockpile. Those large dishes for planned leftovers save on cooking and prep time, virtually giving you a night or two off every week.

Planning your weekly meals is easy when you know the basics, and soon you'll be saving time and money while creating menus with care, giving you and your family the nutritional value you deserve on a fast-food budget. You don't have to spend a lot to be healthy; you just have to plan ahead. I'll show you how.

Planning a Day Ahead

The first thing to do is to commit to planning your menus. Everybody likes the *idea* of menu planning, but it's far too easy to put off, waiting for that magical moment when we are much more organized and have the leisure time to sit down and work it out. The truth is that making a menu will save you time in the end (and possibly make you feel like you're just a little more organized). If you're new to menu planning, there are some easy ways to get started. One of my suggested methods requires only that you plan each meal the night before. This plan has the most flexibility, but doesn't take much strain off of shopping time or the budget. Still, it's a big step toward familiarizing yourself with your own pantry and will help you focus on buying only what you need.

First, let's break down what goes onto your plate. You'll want to have a protein, a starch, and a vegetable or fruit side. The protein ranges from the traditional beef, poultry, fish, or pork to beans and tofu. Pasta, rice, and potatoes are some typical go-to starches, and salad, veggies, or fruit are recommended to round out a healthy meal. Breads, such as rolls and biscuits, are optional, as are desserts. You can make dessert healthy by having fruit instead of something sugary or high in fat. Try to avoid completely new meals when you first get started with meal planning. Instead, incorporate new foods in with familiar ones to avoid a negative reaction from others in your household.

Start by making a list of meals that you've made in the past or that you've been wanting to try out. Think of casseroles (which are great for making ahead and even freezing) and dishes that call for money-saving ingredients like ground beef and chicken. Take your time and plan carefully—you'll be glad you did. If your list seems too short, don't worry, you'll be able to add to it as you discover more recipes. Once you've got a list going, scan through it and check the dishes that are the most budget-friendly. These select meals will be a master list that you can use for easy reference in the future.

As you plan your meals, make sure to get the input of the rest of your household. It's always a bad idea to buy food that you know won't get eaten. Don't waste your money.

Planning a night before is easy: just take a few minutes to look at what you have on hand and think about what you can make with those items. Check the fridge thoroughly for food that will soon expire, and investigate your pantry and cabinets well. Start with fresh produce and dairy and work to the dry grains and canned food. It will take some getting used to, but over time, you will be able to whip something up from nearly bare cupboards like a pro.

Planning a Whole Week

Thinking about meals a day ahead is very helpful and reduces costs by removing impulse buys and fast food from the equation, but doing it every day may get tiresome. Luckily, once you've got the hang of planning a day in advance, it's easy to take the next step to outlining a week's worth of meals in one planning session.

Let's start with a weekly plan that's quick and easy: seven little dinners for seven days in the week. You don't need to do a whole inventory list, index all your ingredients, and plan a stockpile expansion; it's just a few meals. And once you master this, you'll be so in tune with your inventory that planning for a month will be a snap. But slow and steady wins the race, so let's stick to a week for now.

While nightly planning is helpful for using up the food you have on hand, weekly planning gives you a real edge at the grocery store. Take a look at the weekly circulars in your paper or on your markets' websites. See what kind of specials and bargains there are and let those be your guide for this week's dinners. If you find a great deal on chicken, plan for Oven-Fried Chicken (page 140), Southwestern Supreme Chicken Soup (page 136), or Slow Cooker Chicken Alfredo (page 128). Seasonal items and loss leaders—items stores promote on sale so that you'll buy other regular-price items while you're shopping—are going to be your best bets in produce and meats. Plan to take advantage of these low prices without going for the related marked up items. This is something you'll often see around holidays and festive occasions. A headliner like turkey might be a steal, but the cranberry sauce and Stove Top stuffing are suddenly higher in price.

Okay, the grocery store ads are here and it's time to sketch out a rough menu plan. Here are the basics of minimizing cost and time in the kitchen while shopping for seven meals:

- ❧ Break each meal into three parts: an entree, a side, and a salad. That's twenty-one menu items.

- ❧ Create a list of ingredients you have in your pantry, stockpile, or fridge that need to be used up and assign them categories. Make a shopping list of items you need to fill in the blanks and complete the menu.

- ❧ Shop with an open mind. Stick to your list, but don't just grab what you came for if you see a better, unadvertised bargain. Keep an eye out for better deals and be ready to make substitutions.

- ❧ Flesh out your menu plan while you put away your groceries. Plan your quick meals for busier nights based on your family's calendar.

- ❧ Post your menu plan on the refrigerator door and refer to it during the week.

- ❧ Give yourself a high five!

You did it! You made a plan and stuck to it. You shopped from a list while retaining flexibility and put together a great menu for a week's worth of dinners. Those are the basics, but why stop there? Here are five little hints that will help you perfect the art of menu planning as you hone your new skills:

1. *Build a shopping list that reflects you.* A blank list can beg for unneeded ingredients or, worse yet, it could stay blank. Start your weekly shopping list with a predetermined set of items that you and your family like to eat. Be realistic about your family's habits, but leave room for positive dietary changes, such as picking up some fresh produce, substituting complex carbohydrates for simple ones, and trying out lean proteins. Be sure to include herbs, spices and sugar, flour, and other staples to have on hand. When you've got it down, print fifty-two copies of the list and tear through those sheets throughout the year like you would a hilarious desk calendar. As you plan your meals, circle the items you'll need to purchase and be sure to post the lists on the fridge, so when somebody uses up a carton of milk or a box of cereal they can circle it on the list as well. Things that get used get bought, while poor impulse buys that languish on the shelves do not get replaced.

2. *Find your routine and understand your own weekly schedule.* If work and play don't map your destiny for you, then plan your meals around the amount of time you care to spend the kitchen or finishing leftovers from the previous night's dinner. Create a taco or casserole night and have a specific night

of the week for grilling or sandwiches. It's always great to work a "Cook's Choice" night into your weekly routine, when you can throw something together based on whatever's left in the kitchen the night before grocery shopping. You'll get really good at creating salads and stir-fries out of whatever's in the fridge and making use of neglected leftovers. Don't forget the freezer either. You may be sitting on all the ingredients for a meal and save yourself a trip to the store. By introducing this weekly habit into your routine it will become a built-in part of your everyday life.

3. *Stay flexible when routines get broken.* Unexpected changes don't have to result in costly fixes. Just swap menus for a quick solution and edit your schedule to meet the circumstances. It's a good idea to always have a couple of safety meals on the plan for just such an occasion. Leftovers from bulk meals are one way to help with this, or even allowing yourself a pizza night or fast-food run. If you're accustomed to visiting a drive-through for your dinner, don't try to quit cold turkey. It can be a difficult transition, so don't let that to keep you from making any changes altogether. Keep a night for fast food in your arsenal if you aren't completely comfortable with your planning and eliminate it when your routine is more solidified.

4. *Recycle your menu plans.* Organize recipes by main ingredient so you know just where to look when deals pop up. After a while your file will grow and break down into other categories, like meals for warm or cold weather. Try to assemble six to eight menu plans for each season. This keeps just enough variety in

your routine. Ground beef can be burgers, burritos, spaghetti, or cabbage rolls depending on the season. So when beef goes on sale, you'll have a go-to plan no matter what time of year! After you've amassed an arsenal of menus on file, you can make the move from weekly to monthly planning without breaking a sweat. When you know how your kitchen and inventory work, it only requires a few more minutes to draw up a plan for three extra weeks and stretch your storage muscles by fully utilizing the pantry and the freezer.

5. *Have easy meals ready.* The unplanned trip for takeout is bad for the budget, but let's get serious: there are simply some days when you don't want to cook an elaborate meal. This is why you need some supersimple meals in your arsenal that can be whipped up in a jiff. Dried pasta and bottled pasta sauce are a great example: frugal, simple, long shelf lives, perfect when you don't want to cook.

Keeping Menus Spicy

It sounds familiar. Meatloaf on Wednesdays, Taco Tuesdays. It may seem boring, but the reliability of having the same menu plan every week is highly convenient. But if your family is balking at the idea of another tuna noodle casserole, it's time to rotate your menu. You can spice things up week to week with these tips for taking your routine dinner from drab to fab.

Do some impulse shopping. You know they say rules are meant to be broken? Head to the store and walk the baking and ethnic foods areas for a little bit of inspiration. You can also use fresh produce to change things up or get an idea from the cover of a frozen entree similar to one of your stock recipes.

Swap a side. Again, the produce section is a great place to find new ingredients for a salad or side. The deli section or salad bar of your store will also give you ideas for salads and sides. Look for dishes that use similar ingredients to put into your well-oiled routine.

Feed your head. Whatever the main ingredients, there are countless ways to prepare them, and lots of inspiration is available in cookbooks or online. The same staples don't have to taste the same every week. Keep learning new spins on all of your tried and true dinners.

Buying in Bulk

Rotating menus can be real time-savers and don't have to be boring. But the effectiveness in cost-saving varies, as the planning is not based on current prices and doesn't account for the changing status of your stored food. That is where buying in bulk and optimizing your storage comes into play.

The Pantry

The first storage goal is to build your pantry knowledge. When you plan menus by the month, storage naturally takes on a more important role. By now, your routine should have you using what you put in your pantry and not letting it go to waste. Start by labeling everything you've got on hand and keeping an eye out for nonperishable sale items that will work with your meal plans. Don't forget to label bulk items when you get home from the store! Bags of grains, beans, and other staples from the bulk bins often come home with little more to identify them than an indecipherable number. A great price on flour does you no good when you can't remember if it's bread flour or gluten-free.

The Deep Freeze

When your pantry is in tip-top shape, the next thing to do is feed your freezer. The freezer is great for keeping things fresh longer, but it's not just for raw meat and veggies. You can make one night of cooking last for a whole month if you use your freezer properly. Make your own frozen entrees. Burritos and enchiladas work particularly well. You can also stop skipping breakfast on rushed mornings by preparing egg and sausage burritos in advance. Using the freezer to bank your meals saves time and money by letting you buy in bulk and limit the use of kitchen appliances.

Freezer Cooking for a Month of Meals

Congratulations! You've mastered your menu plans, whipped your kitchen into shape, and conquered the bulk aisle at the grocery store. Now we're cooking with fire, or, I should say, cooking with ice. We've talked about using the freezer for storing both staple ingredients and prepared meals. Now it's going to become your most valued kitchen assistant as we stuff it with meals for a whole month.

WHAT'S SO GREAT ABOUT FREEZER COOKING?

Besides the liberation from your kitchen that freezer cooking has to offer, it promotes nutrition by providing a steady, convenient supply of nourishing, home-cooked meals and eradicates the need for fast-food fixes. Cooking all of your meals at once makes use of the efficiency of an assembly line by grouping like tasks, decreasing your total labor. Buying in bulk lets you save on the total cost of each meal. Heard enough? Let's go!

Start by turning your dining room into your war room. Clear the table and get ready to strategize. The first thing you need to do is to set aside a day for shopping and a day for cooking. A freezer-cooking session uses the same menu-planning skills as any other meal, but the focus is on meat, at least to start. Sit down with a stack of index cards and the weekly grocery store ads, and start flipping through to find the specials. Label an index card for each cut of meat that's on sale: ground beef at the top of one, pork loin on the next, and chicken thighs on another. Think of the entrees each cut of meat suggests and write them down on the card. You may go back to the ads later to round out your menu, but now take your cards and locate the recipes for the dishes you've written down. This may take some time, but it's totally worth it. Using cooking software with shopping list and menu plan functions is a great way to do this, but I find that large index cards are very useful for shopping lists, recipes, and meal planning.

Just as with weekly menu planning, keep track of key events on your calendar and maintain variety. Mix simple reheat jobs with fancier meals to account for all occasions. Mark up your calendar with the nights you won't be in, and plan to go out for dinner on your cooking day. You've just cooked a month's worth of meals— you deserve it! When the month is planned out, post your calendar of meals on the fridge to refer to throughout the month.

For your shopping list, be sure to include the correct quantities. Compare your list to what you already have and make adjustments. Once you've bought the rest of the ingredients, make sure you have your recipes at your disposal. Group the recipes with similar steps together; don't, for example, chop onions three separate times for three separate recipes. Put the common prep steps together.

Now it's time to cook, cook, cook (and then freeze, freeze, freeze). There's no getting around the fact that this is a lot of work, but by prepping your ingredients together, you're handling your recipes much more efficiently. When you're done, you'll have a month of meals all worked out with no more shopping or food prep. Enjoy! Now, who's ready for takeout?

SMALL FREEZERS

Maybe a month's worth of meals is too optimistic. That's okay. There are packing techniques that will help you maximize space, but to start, let's try a two-week plan. If you are new to cooking, a two-week plan is a lot more manageable while you build your chops. And even small freezers are capable of storing two week's worth of food. To store your food, make each entree as flat and compact as possible in a zipper-seal freezer bag. Let as much air out as you can. And a little housekeeping goes a long way: if there's a frostbitten ice cream carton or unlabeled bag of... something? Something greenish? Time to free up some space.

Calculating Costs

Sticking to a budget is great, but learning how to decrease your budget is even better. Calculating your cost per meal will help you make informed decisions when planning future menus. You may find that you can spend even less on groceries, or you may learn that you can buy better ingredients for the same amount that you're paying now. Coming up with the per-meal cost also sheds light on the price difference between home cooking and fast food, delivery, and dining out. All this menu planning and time spent in the kitchen may seem like a big pain, so calculating costs is a great way to determine its real value.

Start with the amount you spend on groceries in a week. Let's say $72, just as an example. Divide that number by the number of people you feed every week. If there are three people in your house, that means each person costs $24 to feed that week. At three meals a day and with seven days in a week, each person has about twenty-one meals. Divide that up and it's about $1.14 per meal!

A dollar and change per meal sounds great, but maybe $72 doesn't represent your entire food cost for that week. Sure, you bought in bulk and looked out for sales, but you also used ingredients you already had on hand (and paid for in weeks past), and there was that trip to the farmer's market.

Don't worry about it. Just keep saving your grocery receipts and calculating your costs each week. As time goes by, your calculations will eventually include those weeks when you stocked up steaks for the freezer and the ones when you just needed a few items to round out your pantry stockpile. Once you've got a few weeks of calculating under your belt, you can average them to find out how much you paid for each meal over a whole month. This will give you a great idea of how your shopping and cooking habits are stacking up against dining out or fast food.

Once you've got a handle on planning your dinners for a night, a week, or a month, you'll find that lunch and breakfast rely on the same principles. Breakfast is the simplest, requiring very little variety (if any). Lunch may need some planning, but a simple sandwich and side of soup or a salad can often be pulled together with the same ingredients you're already buying for dinner. And there are always leftovers!

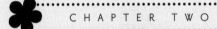

CHAPTER TWO

The Grocery Store

When you go grocery shopping, there are few things
you need: money, your coupons, and a list. No list?
Then stop right there. Think of your list as your weapon
in battle—the grocery store battle.

The following are my top twenty-five strategies for smart shopping. Stick to these tips and you will save money, money, and your sanity.

1. *Don't shop hungry.* I have broken this rule before and the results were not pretty. It's common sense: everything sounds delicious when you're hungry. Chances are you'll impulsively buy all kinds of tempting snacks, none of which were on your list (or within your budget). I always have gum on me when I go shopping, so if I suddenly get a hunger attack I have something to "munch" on.

2. *Budget like no one's business.* Because you made a list, you should have a clear idea of what you'll need to spend. This is your budget: write the dollar amount down and try to stick to it. Of course, one's budget should be somewhat flexible—you never know what hot clearance item you may find. And if you come home under budget, transfer the remaining amount into your "splurge jar."

3. *Running out of something? Write it down.* What do you do when you're on your last bag of Chex Mix? Write it down. If I've learned anything from my years of strategic grocery shopping, it's leave NOTHING to memory. Making a note of dwindling kitchen staples is extremely helpful when you are developing your shopping list and budget. I keep a small notebook in the kitchen—quick and easy.

4. **Buy frozen vegetables.** This strategy has saved me so much money. Frozen vegetables are much cheaper than fresh and most times are easily interchangeable in recipes. And, of course, frozen vegetables have a much longer shelf life.

5. **Pantry checklist.** This is a MUST. Make a checklist of everything you have in your pantry and how much. I write in pencil so I can easily amend the list as I used up my stock. This way, you'll know when you've run out of something and need to add it to your shopping list. This also eliminates the problem of buying duplicates of something you already have.

6. **Pack it yourself.** Some of the most overpriced things at the store are premade snacks—especially cut vegetables and fruit. I make it a rule not to buy any prepared foods that I cannot easily make myself. So get those baggies and start chopping.

7. **Buying in bulk.** For things that you use constantly—say, peanut butter—it's smarter to buy in bulk to decrease the overall cost per ounce. But don't go overboard. Personally, I know I go through food phases. The worst thing to do is buy five pounds of peanut butter and find out that no one in your family wants to eat it.

8. **Check out the specials.** Grocery store ads (in print and online) usually come out on Wednesdays. But this is a tricky tip, because you don't want to be enticed into buying something you don't need. If you don't need it, then don't buy something just

because it's on sale. Bonus Tip: Many stores have unadvertised specials—you can usually find these on the higher and lower shelves.

9. *Shop at the right time.* I have made the mistake of shopping at the wrong time on too many occasions to count. Avoid the after-work hour on weekdays, Fridays, Sunday evenings, and major holidays. Personally, I like shopping in the morning, when I find the shelves are better stocked and can take the time to get everything on my list while keeping an eye on my budget.

10. *Keep your eyes on the prize.* You're more likely to buy something that grabs your attention. This is why stores place displays in the aisles—they are meant to stop traffic. Just a few seconds of your consideration makes an impact on whether or not you buy. Do yourself a favor and try to give most of your attention to your list and not the dazzling display of sugary cereals at the end of aisle five.

11. *Avoid convenience stores.* All of that so-called convenience comes at a price. A really, really high price.

12. *Know when to ditch the cart.* If you are just running to the store for a few things, then don't use a cart. Skip the basket too if you don't need it. You don't want to be induced to buy more. Limiting to the amount you can carry will help you stick to your list.

13. **Ask questions.** I know the delivery schedule for fresh fruits and vegetables at my local market. Since these items go bad so quickly, it's smart to get them as fresh as possible. How do I know when the perky new produce is coming in? I asked!

14. **Rain check, please.** If the sale item you're searching for is no longer in stock, ask for a rain check. When the item is back in stock, you can snag it for the sale price.

15. **Compare, compare, compare.** One big mistake shoppers make is buying the largest package thinking that it is the most cost-effective. Sometimes this is true, but not necessarily. At most stores, you can see the price per ounce on the price tag on the shelf—knowing this has really helped me save money.

16. **Be on the edge.** The perimeter of the store is where all the good stuff is, including baked goods, produce, dairy, and meats. The reason for this is grocery stores want you to have to walk as much as possible. Keep in mind that you might not have to wander every aisle to find everything you need.

17. **Check that receipt.** Take a minute or two to make sure that all your items and coupons were scanned correctly. I have found that sale items don't always scan at the correct price. A quick once-over after each shopping trip could save you a pretty penny.

18. **Loyalty is for the dogs.** Maybe you have a favorite brand of mustard, but why? Next time, try the one that's on sale. Re-

member to look at the unit price to spot the best deal. You may even end up liking one of the less-expensive brands.

19. Try generic. I am almost always a fan of the store's house brand. Many times, the store brand is equal in quality to the name brand, but without the hefty price tag. Just give it a whirl.

20. Couponing. We'll talk about everything coupons in Chapter Six. But it's important to know when to use them. Having a coupon for a something doesn't mean you have to buy it.

21. Clearances. This is one of my favorite ways to save at grocery stores. Clearances (or "manager specials") are found throughout the store, but usually in the back. This is where you can snag day-old bread for a fraction of the cost. Many items in the clearance section still have long shelf lives but because of some circumstance—a dent in the can or impending sell-by date—the store cannot sell them at their full retail price. There is usually a high volume of clearance items in the meat and produce sections.

22. Strategizing your shopping list. You most likely shop at the same store frequently. Organize your shopping list by aisle so you can easily find the items that you are looking for. Zigzagging back and forth across the store can add a lot of time to your shopping trip.

23. Use a grocery price list. A grocery price list is a list of items you use the most and how much you normally pay for this item. This will help you spot bargains and avoid overpaying.

24. Go shopping alone. Shopping alone allows you to focus on the task at hand. It has been noted that people buy more when they are shopping in groups.

25. Clean that fridge. Make sure to go through your fridge at least once a week. Knowing what you have in your fridge means knowing what you need to buy.

Saving Money on Produce

Some items in the grocery store rarely have coupons—one of them is produce. Below are some great tips and tricks to reduce your produce bill.

Buy seasonal. This is a must. In-season produce is much more likely to be grown close to home. Why does this matter? Those rock-hard peaches you'll find at the store in December came from a distant land with a warmer climate. The price you pay includes the cost of shipping that fruit thousands of miles from Mexico or South America. You'll find that in-season produce that didn't spend months in cold storage tastes much better anyway.

Find a local farm to pick your fruit. Not only is it tons of fun, but it is often cost-effective. When you find a great price, you can stock up and freeze the fruit for later.

Weigh it. Always make sure to weigh your produce before you tie off that bag. This will help you gauge the impact of your product purchase on your budget.

Check that clearance shelf. Most stores have a section where they place produce on clearance. These fruits and veggies are on the edge of being past their prime, so if you do pick some up, make sure to have a recipe ready or be prepared to freeze. Items like overripe bananas are great for smoothies and banana bread.

Check for coupons. There are occasionally coupons for produce—usually for well-known brands like Dole. I find most of my produce coupons in the produce section itself, so keep your eyes open.

Did you know that you can use coupons on clearance items? For example, if Dole bagged salad retails for $2.99 and was placed on clearance for $1.50, and you happen to find a coupon (either a peel-off coupon on the package or on a tear pad in the produce section) for $1 off, you'll be able to grab that salad for only 50¢.

Farmers' markets. Some of the best produce is found at farmers' markets, but timing is everything. The best time to go to the farmers' market is right before it closes—you have huge bargaining power at this time. Everything that hasn't sold must be transported back at the risk of getting damaged. Most farmers will be happier to sell the produce at a lower rate than take a complete loss.

Can it. You can always use canned or frozen fruits and vegetables instead of fresh. I actually prefer buying produce this way, mainly because it's picked at its peak of ripeness. Frozen produce retains many of its vitamins and minerals and can be much more convenient to use.

Grow it. Growing your own food is so rewarding—but it is not easy. If you are new to gardening, start with some easy vegetables like peas, squash, radishes, and spinach.

Watch for sales. If there is a sale on produce, make sure to stock up. Different fruits and veggies go on sale each week. Keep this in mind when creating your meal plan.

Swap colors. Orange and yellow bell peppers are much cheaper than red, but essentially taste the same. You can save some money just by swapping out a red pepper for an orange or yellow one.

Saving Money on Juice

Refrigerated juice. This is the most expensive type of juice in the store. The good news is that there are always coupons available for this type of juice. So make sure to pair a coupon with a sale to maximize your savings.

Frozen juice. I love stocking up on frozen juice, mainly because it's less expensive and more convenient than fresh is. Look for a generic brand or wait for a sale to pair with a coupon.

Bottled juice. There are frequently coupons from major companies like Ocean Spray and Langers. Avoid paying more than $1.50 per quart for bottled juice.

Saving Money on Milk

Finding coupons for milk is rare, but this doesn't mean you can't save a pretty penny. Below are some easy ways to slash the price of this diet staple.

Go big. Quarts and pints cost more per ounce than larger containers of milk. But consider how much milk you go through. Try to buy as much milk as you would use in five to six days.

Go to the gas station. This is actually one of my best tips! More often than not, gallons of milk are cheaper at gas stations than the grocery store. Keep your eyes peeled while you're filling up your tank.

Price match. Look through the weekly ads. Almost every store will list their milk prices for the week.

Make it instant. Instant nonfat dry milk costs less per serving than fresh milk, and it's perfect for use in cooking and baking wherever milk is called for—you really can't tell the difference. You can also mix instant milk (prepared with water) with fresh milk to maximize your use of the fresh milk; just combine them in a one-to-one ratio.

Go generic. Most stores have a house brand of milk—the taste and quality is the same as the expensive brand.

Buy marked down milk. Clearance to the rescue again. Keep your eyes open for markdown tags. Because milk has such a short shelf life, there's a good chance of finding markdowns on a regular basis. Take a few minutes to talk to the person who stocks the dairy section and ask for the best time to snag milk on clearance. Asking a couple questions could save you a good deal of money.

Freeze it. When my husband was single, he did this all the time to lengthen the life of the milk he bought. If you find a great deal on milk, you can stock up and freeze it. Please note that this only works with skim milk. When you want to use the milk, let it thaw in the fridge. The texture of thawed milk may have changed a little, but it's fine for use in recipes.

Watch the expiration date. The worst is having to throw milk away because you let it go past its expiration date. When you buy milk, try to get a carton with the expiration date farthest out. I find it helpful to write the expiration date on the milk cap once I get home. If you notice that the expiration date is approaching and there is no way you will be able to use up all the milk in time, then freeze it.

Request coupons from milk companies. You can e-mail a milk company about their products, and there is a good chance they'll send you a coupon. You can also check out company websites to see if they have any printable coupons. Here are a couple websites that have coupons to print:

- ❈ SilkSoyMilk.com
- ❈ ShamrockFarms.net
- ❈ OrganicValley.coop

You can also follow companies on social networking sites like Facebook and Twitter, where they often announce promotions and post coupons.

Saving Money on Cheese

Cheese is a staple in most households; however, coupons for and sales on cheese are rare. Below are some easy ways for you save on this yummy product.

Do the math. Blocks of cheese vary in size; make sure you are looking not so much at the price tag but at the cost per ounce. The smaller the amount of cheese, the more likely the higher the cost per unit.

Grate it up. This is such a simple way to save some money. The cost per ounce of pre-shredded cheese is higher than that of block cheese. Moreover, there are extra preservatives added to the pre-shredded cheese to keep it from clumping. To save money and avoid unnecessary preservatives, I grab the block cheese and grate it at home. To make softer cheeses easier to grate, put them in the freezer for about an hour.

The same goes for pre-sliced cheese. Do your own slicing and save money. Did you know that bulk cheese is actually better for you, with more calcium than pre-sliced or individually wrapped cheese?

Make it strong. Using a stronger cheese in your recipes means more flavor for less money. Try subbing a sharp cheddar in for more mild Colby.

Freeze it. Freezing cheese allows you to take advantage of good prices and stock up on staples like cheddar and mozzarella. Freeze any cheese that you won't use right away in tightly sealed plastic bags. It's a good idea to cut large blocks of cheese into more moderate portions before freezing so you can defrost exactly as much as you need.

Watch out! For your hard-earned dollars, you probably want the real thing and not imitation cheese. Much of the cheese sold at Walmart is imitation cheese. Not only does this product not taste like real cheese, it really doesn't melt well.

Make ends meet. This tip takes a little bit of work. Look for leftover cheese ends (your local deli counter should have some). They are sold at a steeply discounted price. The ends are perfect for recipes with a cheese sauce, like mac and cheese.

Saving Money on Meat

This is where I get the most questions. Since there aren't many coupons for meat, people think it's hard to save on this staple. Below are some helpful tips for spending less on meat.

Know what you're paying for. When buying meat, compare the cost per serving instead of the cost per pound. A piece of boneless meat may be a better buy than a cut at a lower price per pound that has lots of fat and bone.

Markdowns. Again, clearance is your friend. Most stores mark down meat prices at night or early in the morning. Meat does not have a long shelf life, so something is always going on clearance. Be on the lookout for stickers announcing "Buy One, Get One Free." If you snag an unexpected deal on clearance meat, you can always freeze it. Just make sure to pack it well to avoid freezer burn.

Lunch meat. Before going to the deli counter, check out the packaged lunch meat. There are often coupons for the prepackaged meat.

Go to the deli. If you can't find a good deal on pre-sliced lunch meat, then hit up the deli counter and have your meat sliced. That way you can buy as much or as little as you need.

Lower your standards. Consider buying lesser cuts of meat (like chuck), then tenderizing, marinating, or slow cooking them. Less-expensive cuts of meat are just as nutritious as their more tender counterparts and, cooked right, they can be just as delicious.

Get the whole chicken. Buying the chicken whole and cutting it into parts yourself is an easy way to save money.

Leave the store. Consider buying meat from your local butcher shop. Though there's no guarantee that prices will be lower, it doesn't hurt to check.

Change the color. Instead of buying red meat, try less-expensive chicken or turkey. Both chicken and turkey contain more protein and less fat than many other meats.

Make it a family affair. Family-sized packages are often cheaper than individual pieces of meat. Don't forget to freeze anything you're not going to use right away.

Hit the ground. Ground beef is a good buy since it is fairly lean. Less fat means a higher meat yield after cooking. Ground beef also freezes very well.

Make it last. Using meat in every meal can become costly. These days, I'm using less meat and loading up on high-protein foods like legumes. Grains like pasta and rice can really round out a meal.

Stay away from boneless chicken. Though skinless, boneless chicken breasts are perfect for easy cooking, they are very expensive. Save money by buying bone-in chicken instead; it's much cheaper and you can remove the skin yourself.

Think outside the box. Say you're having trouble finding a good deal on fresh fish. Instead of blowing your budget at the meat counter, why not check other sections of the store for canned or frozen fish? The freezer aisle has a fair selection of fish and meat—much of which you can save on with coupons.

Use it all. Don't throw away that leftover roast chicken. Take off the leftover meat for use it in a soup or casserole.

Saving Money on Bread

Head to the clearance. This is the first place I go at the grocery store. There is almost always a good selection of bread. Though not freshly baked, this bread is still fine for at least a day or two. Well wrapped, bread also freezes well. And if your loaf goes stale, not all hope is lost:

How to Refresh Stale Bread

❄ Set oven to 350°F.

❄ Place bread in a brown paper bag and close tightly.

❄ Lightly wet the outside of the bag with cold water and place on a cookie sheet.

❄ Bake 5 minutes for rolls and 20 minutes for larger loaves.

Get creative. There are infinite uses for stale bread. Croutons, bread pudding, and French toast are all great ways to use up a loaf that's past its prime. Stale bread can be used to thicken stews and leftover bread crumbs can go in burgers or stretch a meatloaf.

How Stores Get You to Spend

Everyone knows about the temptations of the checkout counter impulse-buy: candy, gossip magazines, and more candy, all staring you down while the shopper ahead of you digs through her purse for exact change. But did you know that grocery stores use dozens of other tactics to entice you to buy? Below are some of their top tricks for getting you to spend more time and, therefore, more money in the store.

The shopping cart. Introduced in 1938, the now-familiar rolling basket was designed to let customers purchase in volume more easily.

High margins. Many grocery stores are designed the same way. Do you ever wonder why flowers and baked goods are some of the first things you see when you walk in the door? Store owners want you to encounter those high-margin items when you have an empty cart and high spirits. Also, both flowers and baked goods have pleasant smells that activate your salivary glands, which is known to increase your chances of making an impulse buy.

Hiding the essentials. Grocery stores hide staples like butter, eggs, and other basics so shoppers have to travel to every corner of the store to get through their lists. By your third march down aisle five, that box of brownie mix or bucket of licorice might look too good to resist (again).

Creating a flow. Most grocery stores move customers from right to left. Because of this flow and our habit of driving on the right side of the road, the items they most want you to buy will be on the right hand side.

Eye level. The items that stores most want to sell are at eye level. The most expensive, name-brand cereal, for example, will float right in front of your face, while products with a lower profit margin are on the lowest shelves.

Mommy, can I have this? Not all eye levels are created equal. Just as there is eye-level product placement for you, products aimed at children are placed at their eye level. This is where they'll find Easy Mac, sugary cereals, and gummy snacks to pick up and beg you to buy.

How does this color make you feel? Packaging design is the product of careful research into what prompts customers to buy. You'll notice many products with red and yellow packaging meant to attract your attention. The fonts, layout, and wording on products are also part of an elaborate dance meant to incite your desire and lure you into buying.

Music to your ears. Music is known to affect people's actions, and slow or classical is thought to make people unconsciously slow down and take their time. Thus, many grocery stores use such music to keep you in the store longer, hoping you'll buy more.

Loyalty cards. Though loyalty cards are a way to save money, their main purpose is to keep you as a regular customer and allow the store to track your spending habits.

Check out...all that candy. The checkout line is known minefield of impulsive buys. Your best bet is to focus on something—anything—other than the nougat-filled candy bars to your right. And left. Try catching up on e-mail on your smartphone or mentally planning tomorrow's meals.

Confusing numbers. Grocery stores use tricky promotions to confuse customers into buying more. Say, for example, jars of tomato sauce—usually $1.99 each—are on special at ten for $10. You might think you have buy ten jars to get the discount. But in almost all cases you don't—it's a sneaky way of saying the sauce is on sale for $1 per jar, and you can buy one, three, or nine jars and still get them for a buck a pop.

CHAPTER THREE

Where to Shop

There's no shortage of places to buy groceries. You may have three or four options right in your neighborhood.

There are the all-in-one superstores, the more common and competitive supermarket chains, farmers' markets, health food stores, and convenient drug stores you probably stop at for emergency items in the middle of the night. Most or all of these places might have everything you need in an average shopping trip, but they vary in convenience, selection, and (of course) price. But visiting each one to look for the best price every time you go out is not an option, unless you've somehow found more than twenty-four hours in the day. So a little bit of research and planning goes a long way toward finding best places to shop.

You Better Shop Around

You won't buy the same brand of spaghetti sauce, laundry detergent, or olive oil if there's a better deal, right? So why would you treat the grocery store any differently than the products it carries? The first step to getting the most out of your grocery store is to make some rounds. Go to each store and compare the prices of staples like milk, cheese, bananas, chicken breast, hamburger buns, and toilet paper. Keep a log of the things you buy and what you pay for them. This log will become your grocery price list, which you'll keep using to keep track of how much you pay for common items on your shopping list. Bring it with you on every shopping trip and refer to it often.

When you shop around, you're doing a couple things. First, by determining the cost of merchandise at each store you visit, you get an idea of the going rate for common products. You'll begin to see which store has the best price and you'll know where to go first for a particular item. You'll also get an idea of each store's inventory. Each store's strengths and weaknesses factor in when you plan your grocery trips.

What's in Store

We talked about the typical market in the last chapter, but these days the grocery store isn't the only place we do our shopping. Here are the benefits and disadvantages of the other places we buy our essentials.

SUPERSTORES

Superstores, like Target and Walmart, are well loved for their one-stop approach to shopping. These days, many have a full-scale grocery store in addition to hardware, apparel, electronics, and everything else you could ever need. It's a great way to knock a lot off the to-do list at once, but it may not be saving you any money. The prices are known to be low and it may be your best bet for things like condiments and frozen or canned vegetables. But superstores are also more focused on boxed and canned products and heavily preserved foods, featuring less fresh produce, meat, and dairy than traditional supermarkets.

HEALTH FOOD STORES AND FARMERS' MARKETS

Though they are typically more expensive, health food stores and farmers' markets offer competitive prices on some items that may surprise you. They're also great for less-common goods that you won't find in other stores. They generally have bulk sections, which allow you to buy in the amounts you want rather than paying for, say, five pounds of whole wheat flour when you only need two cups. It's an option that can help you save money and avoid food waste. Also, the workers at health food stores are frequently more sensitive to special dietary needs and allergies and can help you with questions about unfamiliar ingredients.

DRUGSTORES

Drugstores have great but often confusing reward programs. The hardest thing to comprehend about CVS's ExtraCare or Walgreens's Register Rewards is that they could actually work. Your inner skeptic hears about free products and wants to know what the catch is.

Most stores' rewards programs are based on store coupons that print out on or with your receipt that can be used to purchase just about anything in their store. CVS has ExtraCare Bucks, Walgreens has Register Rewards and more recently have added Balance Rewards, and Rite Aid has +Up Rewards. The premise for each store's rewards programs are similar in the sense that they have you pay a certain dollar amount for an item up front, or out of pocket, and then you may receive the same amount or less back in "rewards," or store coupons. For example, you may be able to purchase Colgate Toothpaste at a sale price of two for $5. Along with that sale CVS may offer an ExtraCare Reward of $4 when you purchase two Colgate Toothpaste items. In this example, you would pay $5 out of pocket, and receive a "reward" of $4 to be used later on almost anything else in the store. If you add to this scenario a manufacturer's coupon for $1 off two Colgate products, you'll have yourself a "free" deal, because you will have paid $4 out of pocket and received a store coupon for $4. Each store has different rules for how their rewards programs work, so it's important to understand the rules for the stores you shop at.

When you get your ExtraCare Bucks for your purchase, you'll understand the benefit of utilizing your local pharmacy for some of your convenience shopping. The money you spend comes back and continues working for you as long as you keep using those rewards. The rewards you receive for buying something like a razor can be used to purchase items that don't normally go on sale, like milk and bread. It's a great way to pay little or nothing for the items you use every day.

It may take time to learn how to spot deals and start getting toothpaste and shampoo for free, but it's possible. Drugstores are the most convenient choice for late-night necessities, but a well-planned trip in daylight hours can net savings on essentials like cosmetics, milk, batteries, and other surprise values.

DOLLAR STORES

Dollar stores are a terrific way to pad your budget by paying less for herbs and spices, kitchen utensils, and cleaning products. Obviously you can't do all of your shopping there, but learn to take advantage of the right bargains. The batteries aren't as good, but drain cleaner and stain remover are a smart buy. I bought an ice cream scoop at the dollar store. It isn't cutting edge scoop technology, but it works just fine for our needs. I've since found scoops at six times the price, but we still use our dollar scoop. Now that's delicious savings.

Making yourself knowledgeable about how prices compare from store to store will save you both time and money. Don't write off an entire store as too expensive. Superstores aren't always cheap. Dollar stores aren't always a good deal. Health food stores aren't always overpriced. Each place has its benefits; you just have to know what they are and how to take advantage of them.

Other Factors That Determine Where You Shop

Coupons. Get an idea of which store will maximize the value of your coupons. Each supermarket has its weekly circulars with their own store coupons. Manufacturer coupons can be used in any store and, paired with the right store coupon, can be an amazing savings tool. I can't tell you how many times I've gone to superstores with a manufacturer coupon, only to find the product either overpriced or absent entirely. What a drag!

Club prices. Examining club prices gives you a good a sense about a store and whether or not they're going to have good deals on the products you need. Soon you'll be able to identify the best savings in the weekly circulars and see where and when your coupons will give you the biggest advantage.

The routine. Part of knowing where to shop is learning your stores' routines and working them into your weekly schedule. Each store has its own way of marking down clearance items. Find the clearance area, usually tucked away on a corner shelf or in a shopping cart. Meats often get marked down on different days at different stores, or at a certain time each day. Some start marking down the meat section at around 5 p.m. each day, so that's a great time to find deals. Just ask your friendly meat department employee when they do the markdowns. You'll be so glad you did.

Your price list. Keeping a price list of the items you buy, familiarizing yourself with what each of your local stores have to offer, and recognizing the advantages and disadvantages of superstores, drug stores, and dollar stores will make you a well-rounded and budget savvy shopper before you even clip your first coupon. You don't have to be a shopping expert before you begin saving. The tricks of the trade are learned on the job. Even with no planning whatsoever, the weekly circulars and store ads are right there when you walk in the door, directing you to the savings. So get out there, get started, and soon you'll notice you are spending less, eating better, and learning to shop smart!

Eating Healthy on a Budget

Eating healthy and saving money are not mutually exclusive, though getting the best of both may require some radical changes in the way you think about food and the way you shop.

You may have some long-held beliefs about the value of a Dollar Meal or the prohibitive cost of organic beef, but you might be wrong!

The Hidden Costs of Convenience

The nutritional information on packaged foods can be grossly misleading. Foods high in sodium and sugar often have a recommended serving size of a third or less of a likely portion. That half a can of Pringles you ate this afternoon? It was three times the recommended serving size, clocking in at 27 grams of fat and 180 percent of your recommended daily sodium intake. This portion-size deception is also used in allegedly healthy frozen dinners. To keep the calories and bad stuff down, they make the serving size so small that you're often left unsatisfied and tempted to fill the extra tummy space with snacks. Cost-wise, if you're buying more food to fill in the gaps that diet food leaves in your appetite, you're spending money on top of the cost of expensive packaged foods.

The cheap menu items at your favorite fast food chain are no better. If you're shelling out for empty calories because you think you can't afford to eat healthy, try paying close attention to how much money you spend weekly on unhealthy foods. Add up receipts from fast food purchases, restaurants, snack stands, and anything you purchase that's loaded with fatty meats, salt, sugar, or oil. Does it still seem like fast food is budget friendly?

You pay for convenience. While fast food is creeping up in price, the value menu still looks cheap in comparison to a grocery bill, not to mention easy. But the truth is that it's cheaper to make a sandwich at home if you shop smart. We want to believe it's cheaper to get fast food because we want fast food; we're used to fast food and don't want to try anything new, particularly if it requires more work. Eating healthy is a commitment, but the notion that a nutritious diet is going to inflate our food budget is fallacy.

Merely stepping into a market doesn't mean you'll automatically start saving money. Preservative-loaded, high-fat, high-calorie processed foods abound at the grocery store. At first, those frozen meals that cost between $3 and $7 each might seem like a smart buy. Compare that to the price of a package of sliced turkey, some cheese, and loaf of bread, which could total up to a $10 meal. Ah, but there's where you're wrong. The value comes from the slices of turkey, cheese, and bread that you'll use to make a sandwich again tomorrow, and the next day, and so on.

The Diet-Friendly Budget

The first step to eating healthy on a budget is merely to have a budget in the first place. Look at how much you spend on food in a month. Don't just count groceries. Account for everything you eat, from fast food, to happy hours, to frozen yogurt to determine how much of your income goes to food. This itemized list will give you a good idea of where most of your food money is going and where you should begin to cut. Notice the relatively high numbers next to those pizza nights and jaunts for Chinese takeout? Try eating healthy for a week and see if you don't spend less.

The Plan of Attack

When focusing on good nutrition, the best parts of the store to pay attention to are the produce, dairy, deli, and bakery sections—all at the perimeter of the market. That's where you'll find all the essentials. The aisles to hit up are the pasta aisle for grains like wheat, rice, and quinoa; the ethnic, or Asian/Mexican foods aisle; the frozen and canned vegetable aisles for certain types of veggies, fruits, and beans; and the baking aisle, which is where you will find the spices, oils, flour, and sugar that you'll use on a regular basis as you put your kitchen to use. If you are near a store with a bulk foods section, where you scoop what you need into a bag and tag it, take advantage of the lower cost per unit on grains, nuts, and dried fruit.

There is one exception to the rule of the outer perimeter: this is often where you'll find the aisle of (decidedly nonessential) beer, wine, and booze. If you have an alcohol budget that's separate from your food budget, you'll have to determine for yourself how much you want to cut back. Buying alcohol at the grocery store is substantially cheaper than going to a bar or restaurant.

And yet, if you spend $15 each week on beer, that could be an easy place to shave $60 per month (or some part of it) from your spending. Drinking water, and lots of it, is one of the best healthy habits to get into, and if you have access to filtered tap water, it's super cost-efficient.

The Building Blocks of Good Nutrition

A healthy diet consists of complex carbohydrates like whole grains, rice, pasta, and bread; fruits and vegetables, which provide your vitamins and minerals; and protein from meats, dairy, and legumes. Protein often forms the cornerstone of every meal, despite the USDA's recommendation that it make up only 20 percent of your diet. Carbohydrates are vital to a healthy diet, though we often get our carbs from simple sources like white bread and pasta rather than fibrous whole grains. Fruits and veggies, the most convenient and natural sources of nutrition, are sadly the most frequently neglected.

The relatively high cost of meat often gives people the idea that fast food is less expensive. You can easily satisfy your meat craving with a Quarter Pounder, but at three bucks, you're still paying $12 per pound. And while you can find meat for far less at the grocery store, eating less meat is actually a great way to eat healthy and save money. Replacing the empty calories of fast food with inexpensive vegetables is a surefire way to save both money and your heath.

If you need that protein fix and can't blow your budget on a good cut of beef, don't start salivating over that processed $6 burger just yet. You get plenty of protein from fibrous whole-grain foods like brown rice, whole wheat pasta, and multi-grain bread. There are hundreds of varieties of beans to choose from, all packing a protein punch. Refried beans are cheap, and dried lentils are also budget-friendly. A dozen protein-packed eggs costs only about two bucks, and even the store-brand egg substitute is a reasonably priced source of protein. Hard-boiled eggs make a portable work or school snack and are great in salads, as are seeds and nuts. Yogurt is another inexpensive source of protein. Three cans a week of tuna or salmon have multiple nutritional benefits, including higher brain function.

Most of these foods are also easier to store than raw meat, as are vitamin-rich frozen veggies, bagged spinach, russet potatoes, and marinara sauce. When you're looking for easy snack food options to replace unhealthy habits, look to the produce section for fresh fruit and vegetables like apples, grapes, carrots, bananas, and oranges. There are so many terrific raw ingredients for building the perfect salad or vegetable soup or for leaving out in a fruit bowl for between-meal snacks. Lemons are terrific flavor enhancers to keep on hand. You'll find it is easy to make many of your own sauces and dressings when you keep an eye out for fresh, healthy food.

Whole grains are the easiest things to shop for, and you may not be taking full advantage of the variety your grocery store has to offer. Rice is cheap, easy to make, incredibly versatile, and good for you. You'll save a lot by buying a bag of rice and mixing in some nuts or veggies and herbs instead of buying the boxes that come with unhealthy seasoning (and loads of salt). Pasta comes in several shapes and grains, including corn and quinoa pasta for those with a wheat allergy. Tortillas and pitas are also sources of carbs and the start of a great Taco Tuesday (or Falafel Friday). Burritos can be healthy when made at home, and they freeze wonderfully. Freezing a bunch of homemade burritos to have on hand and re-heat at your convenience is much cheaper than relying on those dinky freezer-aisle burritos.

Another key to saving money while focusing on a healthy diet is to eat seasonally and buy local. Buying local means you're not paying the added cost of shipping food from another part of the world. Seasonal produce is often lower in price because of its availability. You can even take advantage of low seasonal prices by buying in bulk and canning or freezing some for later. Try roasting some summer tomatoes and then stashing them in the freezer. Come winter, those sweet morsels can perk up pastas and la-sagnas and you'll wonder how you ever tolerated the hard pink globe that passes for a tomato in December.

When you're watching your spending, chances are you're skip-ping the more expensive things with labels like "certified or-ganic," "free range," "chemical free," and "sustainable." But once you're eating less meat in favor of legumes and other healthier (and cheaper) protein sources, you may find that the advantages of buying ethically raised, hormone-free meat is worth the extra cost. If you don't want to spring for organic fruits and vegetables, make sure to rinse them with equal parts vinegar and water, since many pesticides are water resistant. Some organic fruits and vegetables are worth the cost, as their conventionally farmed counterparts carry the most pesticides: apples, bell peppers, blueberries, celery, cucumbers, grapes, spinach, lettuce, nectarines, peaches, potatoes, and strawberries. This list is updated annually by Environmental Working Group and can be found on their website, www.ewg.org.

While shopping at your farmers' market, ask the growers about their crops. It's expensive to become a certified organic farm, and you'll find that many farmers grow their crops without pesticides even if they aren't certified. You can also ask about buying in bulk for a lower price. You can also save a lot of money by planting your own garden. Herbs are a great way to start, and carrots and radishes are also easy to grow. Lemon and orange trees are very convenient to have on hand if you can get them.

The Spice of Life

Remember to add some variety to your shopping cart to avoid boredom with your routine. Always keep some herbs and spices on hand. Butter, cinnamon, cocoa powder, lemons, olive oil, pepper, salt, and vinegar are essential for perking up the recipes in your regular rotation.

Stick to natural, essential, unprocessed foods as much as possible. Whether you snack on a peach and some nuts, make a burrito or a big healthy sandwich, or bake a delicious casserole for the family, your improved diet will make you feel better and your budget will be no worse for wear. What you thought was going to be an expensive way of life actually makes better financial sense. You may even find yourself on fewer trips to that other section of the store that used to take a chunk out of your paycheck: the pharmacy.

CHAPTER FIVE

Coupons 101

By the end of this chapter you will be a Coupon
Master. What is a Coupon Master, you ask? Well, a
certified Coupon Master knows where to find coupons
and how to use them to best maximize her savings.
Let's get started!

The Origin of Coupons

Logically, coupons and the giveaway of free products are a little backward. Think about it: how does giving away a free or hugely discounted product help the company make money?

Did you know that it was Coca-Cola that offered the first coupon in 1888? Coca-Cola issued "Free Product Coupons" for their beverage in magazines and mailers to potential customers, reimbursing in free syrup the vendors who gave away drinks. It was from this revolutionary tactic that Coca-Cola grew at a rapid rate and in seven years was available in every state in the U.S. This promotion ran through 1913, and between 1888 and 1913 one in nine Americans had claimed their free Coke, totaling a whopping 8.5 million drinks.

Let's just say other companies started to notice the success that Coca-Cola was having. Post Cereal followed in 1908 with a 1¢ coupon for their Grape Nuts cereal.

But the real catalyst of coupons' popularity was the Depression. The depressed economy created an increased need for companies to attract customers, and coupons filled the bill. In 1940 the first in-store coupon was used. In-store coupons were used by large grocery store chains to get business away from mom and pop stores.

Why Coupons?

So, why would anyone offer coupons? First, there are two types of coupons: the in-store coupons you get from your local retailer, and the manufacturer coupons that come straight from the company that manufactures the product. An in-store coupon moves inventory and entices savvy shoppers who won't pay top dollar for their products. Retail prices are well above the actual cost of an item to the retailer, so these markdowns still turn a profit and keep merchandise flowing, which means less waste. It really is a win-win situation—when coupons are used correctly.

Manufacturers may distribute coupons for similar reasons, but usually these types of coupons are used for promotions. Gillette may be unveiling a new type of deodorant, or Tide may have a new magic ingredient that removes tougher stains faster. The coupons put out by manufacturers promote brand awareness and get more products into more homes, thus edging out the competition. It's essentially advertising.

So, coupons give manufactures recognition and prowess by putting their products in people's homes. And stores use coupons to get savvy shoppers in the door. But can it really be worth it for businesses when an obsessed couponer can reduce her grocery bill to near nothing? How can stores that double coupons and have other coupon-friendly policies stay in business with such rampant price slashing?

Sadly, some stores are choosing policies that move away from coupons, or at least make it a little harder to walk out with a cartload of free products. This Budget Savvy Diva, however, thinks coupons are always going to be popular for those looking to save, and stores are always ready to compete for our business. It just means that you have to know who's on your side and where you can get your groceries without overpaying. Manufacturer coupons are good almost anywhere and stores get the money for the listed price, so long as it doesn't exceed the cap on the coupon. They also get additional money for processing, which usually comes out to about 8¢ per coupon.

Coupons can have some crazy features depending on the store you shop at. Some stores double coupons, allow you to stack multiple coupons on one product, accept competitor coupons...some even accept expired coupons! These are just a few reasons it helps to know the coupon policies of the stores where you shop. You also need to know your coupons!

What Makes Up a Coupon?

To become a Coupon Master, one needs to know the anatomy of a coupon. Let's take a look at a standard manufacturer coupon:

One important rule to remember before getting tricky with your coupons is that manufacturer coupons can only be used on a one-per-product basis.

A manufacturer coupon is always labeled as such somewhere on the coupon. Sometimes store coupons will claim to be manufacturer coupons even though you can only use them at one store. If it doesn't say it's from the manufacturer, it isn't a manufacturer coupon.

THE ANATOMY OF A COUPON

Other important parts of the coupon are the barcode, image, expiration date, and description.

The Barcode. Barcodes can be broken and misused by unscrupulous shoppers. This diva is not one to encourage such coupon corruption, but one helpful bit of info about the barcodes is that they will begin with either a 5 or a 9. If it's a 5, that coupon can be doubled at a store that doubles coupons. If it's a 9, not so much. On occasion you may encounter a coupon that says it cannot be doubled, though its barcode begins with a 5. This coupon will be automatically doubled by the cash register at the store and will need to be overridden by the cashier to reverse the doubled amount.

The product image. This is what will give you the best idea of what the coupon can be used for. Many coupons are good only for the product in the size and type shown, but if the description says "any one," you may be able to use your coupon to save on a snack-sized box of cookies instead of the family pack. You can save big bucks on smaller items, even get things for free if the store carries that product within range.

If, for example, you have a coupon for $2 off any Johnson & Johnson product and there is a picture of a big bottle of baby shampoo, but you find a small bottle of Listerine for $2 (also a Johnson & Johnson product), you can get the mouthwash for free, as long as the description on the coupon doesn't restrict certain sizes or have a base price for the product.

The description. Some descriptions will indicate that the coupon is good for any "18 oz. box" or "any product over $5." If no such restriction exists, don't let the picture fool you. Sometimes cashiers will try to give you the brush-off if the value of the coupon is more than that of the product and say that it has to be what's pictured on the coupon. This is not true and most stores' coupon policies will say as much.

The expiration date. Pay close attention to when your coupons expire and keep them handy. Often the coupon is not at its most valuable right away. Products may see a substantial price decrease weeks or months after you clip coupons for them. You maximize your savings when you wait for the price to be right.

Again, the most important thing about coupons is understanding the value and the terms of each one. Always be aware of your store's coupon policy and never be afraid to save money.

ADDITIONAL COUPON TERMS

These are some common coupon terms to know:

One coupon per person. One "like" coupon allowed per person. "Like" coupons are the exact same coupons; they do not mean two coupons with different deals on the same product. For example, if you purchased two bottles of shampoo, and had two of the exact same coupon that said "one coupon per person," you can only use one of the coupons unless you have a second shopper, such as your husband or child, along with you.

One coupon per transaction. One "like" coupon can be used in a single "transaction." A "transaction" ends when payment is made and a receipt is provided. Many stores allow multiple transactions per visit. For example, if you purchased a bottle of shampoo and a bottle of conditioner of the same brand, and had two of the exact same brand coupon that said "one coupon per transaction," you can only use one of the coupons in a single transaction. You can come back another day and use the second coupon, or see if your store allows you to do multiple transactions in one store visit.

One coupon per purchase. One coupon can be used per item, and the item is considered to be the purchase. For example, if you purchased ten cans of soup and had ten grocery coupons for that brand of soup, you could use all ten coupons on the same transaction, which is literally ten purchases. If you were only buying one can of soup, you couldn't use two different manufacturer coupons for that single purchase because that would be more than "one coupon per purchase."

Cash value. The coupon's actual worth, usually around 1/100 of a cent.

Sales tax. The coupon will indicate in the consumer's terms if they need to pay sales tax on the item or not.

Where to buy the product. Many coupons will indicate participating stores where the coupon can be redeemed.

Where to find the product. Especially with newer products, there are usually instructions on where in the grocery store to find them.

Basic Rules of Coupons

One use only. Most of the time coupons can be used only once. For example, if you have one coupon for Easy Mac and you want five boxes of Easy Mac, you can't have your one coupon scanned five times. I mean you can try, but all it's going to get you is an eye-roll from the cashier, at best.

Can I copy that? Let's say you have a smokin' hot coupon—the problem is that you have only one. One might want to make a copy of that hot coupon, but this is a huge no-no. It is actually illegal and can get you into some hot water.

Read the small print. All coupons come with some type of usage terms, including the expiration date, eligible products, and whether or not the coupon can be doubled. Doubling a coupon means the amount of your discount is doubled at participating stores (and if the coupon's small print doesn't prohibit it). For example, if you have a 50¢ coupon for a Twix bar, your coupon has the potential to be worth $1—which would equal a free or extremely inexpensive candy bar.

Clearance is the place to be. Did you know that you can use coupons on items you find on clearance? A coupon can even be doubled on a clearance item—just imagine the savings. It is scenarios like this that give couponers a HUGE advantage. Always remember to check the clearance area. Even if you do not have coupons with you, there is still a chance that there will be "peelie" coupons on the products in the clearance area. I've used this method to snag brownie mix for only 25¢.

Earlier I mentioned stacking coupons. Some stores will allow you to combine a store coupon with a manufacturer's coupon to use for the same product. Your store's coupon policy will tell you if they allow this, as well as whether or not they accept competitors' coupons, double coupons, or expired coupons.

Where to Get Coupons

The most well-known way of getting coupons is in the Sunday newspaper, but there are many different ways to obtain coupons (some free and some not). Most likely you will obtain coupons through many different means.

INSERTS IN THE SUNDAY NEWSPAPER

SmartSource, Red Plum, and P&G are three likely coupon inserts found in your Sunday paper. Inserts are not a guarantee and vary by region. It's up to the coupon distribution companies what coupons go where. Not all newspapers carry inserts and so it's important to determine which ones do before you buy. Typically, the distributors will choose a paper that grants them the most exposure, so the bigger papers get better coupons. The number of newspaper inserts varies from week to week, and it is important to note that no coupons go out during holidays, so save your money for the next week.

Different regions of the country receive different coupons or coupons of varying values. Also, sometimes companies like Target will place coupon inserts for their store in the Sunday paper.

So, should you subscribe to a newspaper for the coupons? First, look into how much it would cost to have the Sunday paper delivered to your home. Many Coupon Masters even get multiple subscriptions. Another option is to go out an buy the paper on Sunday mornings, but be sure to check around for the best price. That's right, newspapers can vary in price from store to store. For example, at many Dollar Tree stores the Sunday newspaper is only a dollar, which is vastly lower than other stores.

Before buying your newspaper, check to see that the coupon inserts are in there. You don't want to get home and find out that someone has "borrowed" your savings.

THE GROCERY STORE

Lots of coupons are available right in the grocery store. Here are some places to find last-minute savings:

Blinkies. You've seen these boxes attached to store shelves with little red lights that blink to grab your attention. The coupons they dispense are actually manufacturer coupons, meaning you can use them at another store. But be careful, many times blinkies are used to promote new products that aren't such a good deal. So snag the coupon and keep it in your stash until a better deal comes around. And while it may be tempting to skip around the store collecting coupons like a carousel rider looking for the brass ring, don't bother with coupons for things you don't want or need. Resisting the siren song of unnecessary items is an important part of becoming a Coupon Master.

Hangtags. These are coupons that hang from the products themselves. These are typically manufacturer coupons. Make sure to read all the print, as there may be stipulations for how to use the coupon, like requiring the cashier to physically take the coupon off the product. Many times these coupons are of high value, so keep an eye out for these. But be considerate: taking hangtags off products you aren't going to buy is a crummy thing to do and unbecoming of a true Coupon Master.

Peelies. These coupons are directly attached to the product and you have to peel them off. You might think you can't use this at the time of purchase, but you can! These coupons can be used on the item you find them on or saved for another time. As with hangtags, remember to read all of the terms carefully.

Tearpads. Pads of coupons are typically found near the product they are for. These are usually high-value coupons.

In-store coupon books. Many stores like Target and Walgreens have their own coupon books, usually found at the front of the store where the weekly ads are kept.

HOME MAILERS
Sometimes coupons are sent directly to your mailbox. These coupons are usually part of a promotion that you signed up for previously.

MAGAZINES
Many magazines (especially women's magazines) have coupons in them. *All You* magazine is packed with coupons monthly. It's available exclusively at Walmart, but you can also subscribe and have it delivered to your home!

ONLINE
Printable coupons are becoming a popular source of savings, especially since it is free to snag them (with the exception of the cost to print them). Your use of printable coupons is tracked by your IP address (the computer you use to get them). Your IP ad-

dress is how the website identifies you as an individual, the same way that Redbox promo codes are granted on a per-credit card basis. Almost all online coupons are limited to a set number of times they can be printed out per IP address. Occasionally you'll find that you can print the same coupon multiple times, but not usually.

You may be required to download software in order to access printable coupons. Use caution whenever you download or install something new to your computer and make sure you are going with a reputable source.

Your best source for finding printable coupons is a devoted website such as www.BudgetSavvyDiva.com. Coupons from all over the Internet are posted daily as they become available. Coupons.com is by far the largest coupon database. Coupons vary by zip code and new ones are are added all the time—mostly at the beginning of the month.

Coupon Boot Camp

We've discussed the difference between a store coupon and a manufacturer coupon and how to read coupons. Now it's time to figure out how to use them!

The first step to making the best use of your coupons is knowing which store to take them to. This is based in part on store policy, but regular retail prices factor in, as do the types of things you might find in your store's clearance section. A coupon by itself does not automatically equal savings, and you will save much more money as your skill level increases with practice, practice, practice. Learn to spot a good deal on products so that you can pounce on them when they happen. You'll maximize your savings by combining coupons with the in-store sales that happen every week. Put together a great sale price with a good coupon and you will see a noticeable difference in your grocery bill.

We also talked about the neat tricks you can do with coupons. Stacking a manufacturer's coupon with a store coupon is a great way to bump up your savings. So is shopping where coupons can be doubled. Using nonspecific coupons good for "any product" to find product portions that increase the value of the coupon will help you keep extra bucks from floating out of your purse. You may even be able to take one store's great coupon to a competitor who retails the product for less or use a coupon past its expiration date. The key is to know your store's coupon policy.

Now that we know how to use coupons and where to find them, let's talk a little bit more about what kinds of savings coupons commonly offer.

Discounts. This is the most common kind of coupon. It offers a product at a discounted price. Usually it's a dollar amount, but occasionally it's a percentage. These savings can easily be squandered when used to purchase a product without first assessing the retail price. The couponing techniques discussed in this chapter work best with this type of coupon, but there are many other ways to save even more.

Free products. Ah, the majestic free product coupon. Get your hands on one of these manufacturer coupons and the world is yours. No tricks, no tactics, no hassle. Just read the fine print carefully. Things to look for are:

There is generally a "maximum value" allowed to be given for free. In most cases the manufacturer will indicate what this is on the face of the coupon, and sometimes the store you are at may charge more for the product than the maximum value allowed. For example, if you have a coupon that says, "FREE—One (1) package of any Oscar Mayer Select Hot Dogs (up to $6.50)," a store may actually sell the hot dogs for $6.99. The cashier would have to input the max value of that coupon which is $6.50, instead of allowing it to automatically take off the entire $6.99, which means the hot dogs really aren't free. In order to get the hot dogs for free with this coupon at this store, you would need to wait for them to go on sale.

The other thing to note is where you can redeem the coupon. Some can be redeemed almost anywhere, others at only participating stores that carry their manufacturer's products.

BOGO: Buy One Get One free (or half off). BOGO offers are great if you plan on stocking up, but be careful. Two for the price of one is a great deal only if you really want two. BOGO coupons are not always the most practical and may trick you into spending money that you could have saved, especially if the second product isn't even free. That said, they are a popular type of promotion and can be a tremendous asset when stockpiling certain types of items. Also, there is one pretty nifty trick to do with a BOGO promotion...

Did you know that you can use another coupon with a BOGO coupon? For example, let's say your local grocery was having a BOGO promotion on bags of Chex Mix, which are normally $2. Thus you are able to buy two bags of Chex Mix for $2. Now let's imagine you have a manufacturer's coupon for $1 off a bag of Chex Mix. You can use this coupon with the BOGO deal to get a dollar off a bag of Chex Mix and still get another one for free. In the end you would be paying only 50¢ per bag. That's snacking by stacking!

Some stores may have policies that overrule this couponing strategy. There is not one blanket rule book that all stores follow; still it's a generally accepted way to stack coupons.

OYNO: On Your Next Order. If you have ever heard of a "Catalina," this is it. Named for the Catalina Marketing Corporation that pioneered this technology, these coupons print out of a special machine along with your receipt at checkout, and are generated based on what you bought during that transaction. These deals are often published on the company's website so you can plan your trip accordingly and purchase items that will earn you Catalinas for other items you want. It's easy to mistake them for garbage, but they may make your next trip a little easier on the wallet. Some stores such as CVS will give you store credit with an expiration date, and sometimes give you the option of having the points electronically transmitted, so you don't even have to carry the paper!

eCoupons. These are another way stores and businesses give loyalty points to their customers. This is something you sign up for through stores to receive printable coupons via e-mail. You can find a wide array of participating stores on ecoupons.com. Likewise, you can score manufacturer coupons by e-mailing them, and often they will send you coupons as a thank-you for your interest (and with the hope that you'll try more of their products).

Rain checks. This is something that a store offers in the event that an advertised sale item is not available and the ad had not indicated the limited nature of the product. In the event that you arrive at the store during the sale and the advertised item is sold out, you can request a rain check or a comparable purchase at the same sale price. If a store repeatedly runs out of sale items without notifying customers of the items' limited nature, then refuses to compensate the customer with a rain check or comparable item, it is considered deceptive advertising and should be reported to:

CORRESPONDENCE BRANCH
FEDERAL TRADE COMMISSION
WASHINGTON, D.C. 20580

Rebates. A rebate is like a manufacturer coupon that the store doesn't want to deal with, so they leave the grunt work up to you. With a rebate, you pay full price for something with the knowledge that you will be reimbursed in part or in whole for the purchase. You are usually responsible for claiming the rebate by sending a form in the mail. After a lengthy period (usually six to eight weeks, but sometimes three to six months), you will receive a check from the manufacturer. Sometimes you can pounce on a rebate during another sale or markdown and score high-priced items for practically nothing. If you purchase something with a rebate offer, it's like free money or a tax refund. But don't forget to mail that rebate in! Companies offer steep discounts and free items through rebates because they're counting on the fact that many consumers will neglect to follow through on the offer.

Coupon Scams

There is one more kind of coupon that everyone should know about.

It's the FAKE coupon.

These coupons float around the Internet and can be difficult for the untrained eye to recognize. Using a fake coupon is a federal offense and can come with a seventeen-year prison sentence and a fine of up to $5 million! Luckily, there are some telltale signs to watch out for. The first rule is that if a deal seems too good to be true, it probably is. Expiration date can also be a red flag: if the coupon is really hefty and doesn't expire for six months, then there might be something fishy going on. Usually, legitimate high-value coupons allow the least time to redeem. You should also check for a UPC code. UPCs, or barcodes, are what allow the coupon to be tracked. If the coupon doesn't have one, it's likely fake. Most fake coupons will be found on sites like eBay. Make sure you get your coupons from a trusted site, like www.BudgetSavvyDiva.com.

If you're savvy about your sources, the couponing lifestyle can help you save loads of cash. It's good to be a Coupon Master!

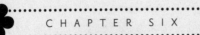

CHAPTER SIX

Creating a Stockpile

As you become a serious, coupon-wielding bargain hunter, you'll begin building quite an inventory in your pantry and freezer. Buying in bulk and taking advantage of sales can save money, but there are tricks to getting the maximum benefit of stockpiling.

What is a stockpile? A stockpile is your accumulation bulk foods, frozen meats and produce, canned goods, and other nonperishables that you can rely on for both your planned menus and your last-minute dinners. Stockpiling is essential for maximizing your savings and avoiding unplanned trips to the grocery store.

Stockpiling is not simply filling up your pantry. Your stockpile should be built on all of the amazing deals you've found through careful couponing, bulk buying, and taking advantage of unexpected deals. The stockpile is an ongoing project and not something you are going to throw together over a weekend. A good rule of thumb is to build your stash from products you've found at a discount of 70 percent or greater.

Stockpiling is a great way to prepare your house for leaner months or even for emergencies.

Consider stockpiling everything you would need to live without electricity for an extended period of time. With this in mind, you should always have drinking water stored. Aim for one gallon per person per day, and make sure to note the water's expiration date.

Getting Started

Couponing, as discussed in Chapter Five, is the best way to start, as it will net you the best discounts on items for your stockpile. Remember to think long term: a stockpile is just for what you're going to use that week, but for months into the future. This is another place where that price book can be tremendously helpful. If you've been keeping track of how much you are paying for certain items, you'll recognize a really low price when you see it. This is the time to snag a large quantity for your stockpile.

How Much Food Do You Need?

Determining how much your family consumes is an important part of knowing how much you should store. For this, menu planning is essential. See Chapter One for everything you need to know about menu planning.

Learn Sale Cycles

It's a little-known fact that grocery sales occur in cycles. Learn those cycles and take advantage of them. I'll bet you didn't know that January is National Oatmeal Month and a great time to stock up on oatmeal. Make sure to ask your local grocer about their sale cycles.

Some common sales cycles include:

January

❊ Oatmeal

❊ Super Bowl treats like soda, dips, crackers, and other snacks

❊ Holiday clearance items like toys, party decorations (think Christmas and New Years), wrapping paper

February

❊ Canned items (fruit, vegetables, and meat)

❊ Valentine's Day goods (including chocolate)

March

❊ Frozen food

April

❊ Ham, eggs, baking goods, butter, and other popular Easter items (don't forget to check after-Easter sales for clearance candy)

❊ Organics (for Earth Day promotions)

May

✿ Barbecue sauce, condiments, chips, grilling meat, and hot dogs for Memorial Day

✿ Chips, salsa, and tortillas for Cinco de Mayo

June

✿ Cheese, cream cheese, butter, yogurt, and eggs

July

✿ Ice cream

✿ Hot dogs, barbecue items like charcoal, chips, and dip for Fourth of July

✿ Back-to-school items

August

✿ More back-to-school items like lunch meat, snacks, and fall clothes

✿ Clearances on summer gear

September

✿ Clearances on back-to-school supplies (this is a perfect time to buy for the next year)

✿ Baby items

October

* Baking goods
* Seafood (October is National Seafood Month)
* Halloween items

November

* Coffee
* Canned goods
* Turkey, stuffing, gravy, and other Thanksgiving items
* Candy and other Halloween clearance items

December

* Party snacks
* Baking goods
* Post-Thanksgiving and -Christmas sales

Where Do I Put All This?

Space may become an issue as your stockpile grows. How do you store a large supply of food without turning your kitchen into a warehouse?

The garage is a common place to use for storage, but not the best area for anything that cannot handle extreme temperatures. Go through your home and look for bulky items that you don't use very often and don't need easy access to. Maybe there are some things taking up important space in your kitchen that can be moved to the garage or under a bed.

Since many items you are stockpiling are used in the kitchen, finding space there is ideal. Sometimes there are unused cabinets in hard-to-reach corners that would make a perfect place to stash items you don't need regular access to (boxes of stuffing and other holiday items, reserves of flour and sugar, unopened bottles of olive oil, etc.).

Some other potential storage spaces include:

Behind Doors. Use a door-hanging organizer to keep snacks and other small items. This is also perfect for bathroom items.

Linen closet. Pillows and linens don't need to take up this important real estate. You can store these items under your bed.

Children's closets. Your children probably aren't using the top shelves of their closets or other out-of-reach storage areas in their rooms.

Bathroom. Clear those redundant chemicals out from under the bathroom sink and use that space for your stockpile of toilet paper, toothpaste, and other bathroom supplies.

Behind cabinet doors. You can really maximize your space in the kitchen by using your cabinet doors for storage. There are racks that mount to the inside of cabinet doors, or you can install magnetized strips to store spice containers.

Under the bed. Heavier items that can stand up to a few dust bunnies, like canned goods, are fine stored under the bed.

Peg-Board with hooks. A great way to store anything that hangs, like batteries, is right on the wall in your garage (or anywhere else you don't mind having a Peg-Board).

Hang it all. A chain mounted from the ceiling may seem unconventional, but add a few hooks and it's a surprisingly efficient way to store bagged snacks and other products, thus freeing up room in your cabinets.

Organizing Your Stockpile

Organization is the key to keeping your stockpile orderly and contained. Having an organization system in place will help you avoid a huge mess as your stockpile grows over time. Make sure you have easy access to your stockpile (even if it's stored in multiple places throughout the house), and that, wherever you store it, it has room to grow.

Plan to rotate the items in your stockpile. All of your time and effort (not to mention savings) will have been for nothing if your supplies go bad sitting on the shelves. Pull the older items to the front and put the newer items you bring home from the store toward the back. When you plan your meals, consider your stockpile before you hit the grocery store. Focus on using up older items before they expire.

Go through your stockpile every three months or so to weed out expired items and see what will be expiring soon. This is also a good opportunity to note which items you aren't going through as quickly; if you find yourself with a surplus of expiring Easy Mac, then maybe it's time to take that off your shopping list (no matter how good the coupons are).

Keeping like items together makes easy to take inventory. Line items one behind the other. Using a label maker and plastic bins lets you group like items that are usually difficult to stack. Clear containers are also perfect for travel-size items, as well as dry goods like flour, rice, and dried beans.

It's important to keep food and chemicals separated to avoid cross-contamination. Storing cleaning products above your food runs the risk of dangerous chemicals leaking into your edibles. If can't keep them completely separate, store cleaning supplies on the bottom shelves that can't be accessed by children or pets.

THE ANATOMY OF A STOCKPILE

So what goes in a stockpile? Here are some good items to start with:

* Canned fruits and vegetables
* Dry goods like granola and cereal
* Peanut butter
* Baby food and formula
* Powdered milk and potatoes
* Canned soup (look for low-sodium varieties)
* Tuna
* Bottled water (cheaper by the gallon)
* White rice (lasts longer than brown rice)
* Freeze-dried foods (these are lightweight and last for years—look for them at your local sporting goods store or at a military surplus store)

IS IT STILL GOOD?

You never want to ask that question when you're in the middle of cooking dinner. It is important to write the date of expiration on your food, especially bulk items that come home from the store with no label. Use a permanent marker to write the date right on the bag or bin. When organizing your stockpile, make sure all of the expiration dates are visible. For boxes, write the date on the box flap and stack them with the flap facing out. For jarred or canned foods, write the date on the lid and arrange them with the items nearing expiration first.

To give you an idea of how long stored food lasts, here is a list of common stockpile items and the length of time they typically stay good. Remember to use common sense and err on the side of safety when it comes to raw meat.

The Freezer: MEAT AND POULTRY, UNCOOKED

❖ Chicken and turkey: 9 months

❖ Steak (beef): up to a year

❖ Pork chops: up to 6 months

❖ Lamb chops: 6 to 9 months

❖ Roasts (beef): up to a year

❖ Roasts (lamb): 6 to 9 months

❖ Roasts (pork and veal): up to 6 months

❖ Stew meats: up to 4 months

❖ Ground meats: up to 4 months

❖ Organ meats: up to 4 months

The Refrigerator: DAIRY PRODUCTS

✿ Butter and margarine: 6 to 9 months

✿ Soft cheese, spreads, and dips: 1 month

✿ Hard and semi-hard cheese: up to 6 months

✿ Milk and cream: about 3 weeks

Note: Do not freeze eggs in their shells.

The Pantry: DRY GOODS

✿ Baking powder and baking soda: 18 months

✿ Bread crumbs: 6 months

✿ Cereals: 6 months

✿ Dry coffee creamer: 6 months

✿ Flour and cake mixes: up to 1 year

✿ Gelatin and pudding mixes: up to 1 year

✿ Herbs and spices: up to 1 year

✿ Nonfat dry milk: 6 months

✿ Pancake and pie crust mixes: 6 months

✿ Pasta and noodles: up to 2 years

- Potatoes (instant): 18 months
- Rice (white): up to 2 years
- Sugar (granulated): up to 2 years
- Sugar (brown and confectioner's): up to 4 months

Optional Pantry Items

- Chocolate (unsweetened): 18 months
- Canned milk: up to a year
- Coffee (vacuum-sealed): up to a year
- Molasses: up to 2 years
- Nuts: about 8 months
- Oils: up to 6 months
- Peanut butter: unopened up to 9 months, opened up to 3 months (longer in the fridge)
- Salad dressing: unopened up to 12 months, opened up to 3 months in the fridge
- Sauces, condiments, and relishes (unopened): up to 1 year
- Shortening: up to 8 months
- Syrups: up to 1 year
- Tea: 1½ years

Fruits and Vegetables

Commercially frozen fruits will last up to a year in your freezer. Commercially frozen vegetables have a lifespan of only eight months. Canning is a great option for storing fresh fruits and veggies bought in bulk. Consider purchasing a canning machine to store food safely. These days there are many books and online tutorials where you can learn how to safely preserve seasonal bounties by canning them.

Beans

Dried beans, kept free from moisture, can last for several years. This is an excellent (not to mention healthy) way to stretch your money.

Drinks

Most unopened juices last three to five years. If you are unsure of how long your juice will last, contact the manufacturer (there should be a phone number located on the product label).

If you notice that you have items that will expire before you can use them, you can always donate them to a local food pantry.

The important thing to remember when buying in bulk is that a deal is only a good one if you actually use the products that you purchase.

CHAPTER SEVEN

Kids in the Kitchen

By involving your children in the kitchen, you will not only get to spend time with one another, but you'll be teaching them lessons they will carry with them for the rest of their lives.

Cooking develops many different types of skills, including math, science, creativity, hand-eye coordination, and reading. You can also teach your children lessons on safety, nutrition, and organization. The kitchen is full of educational possibilities and is a lot of fun, too!

Part of the Plan

Involve your kids from the beginning of the process by having them help you plan the weekly menu. They can help you look through weekly store ads and make the shopping list. You can use this opportunity to start talking about budgets and have them help search for good sales. Let your child pick a few things to put on the shopping list—this will make them feel like an important part of the process. If your child isn't old enough to read, cut out some pictures from the circular and tape them to a special shopping list for your little one to use at the store.

Now it's time to sit down and pick out some fun recipes. Ask the child if they have any ideas of what they want to cook. If needed, you can steer them toward a more nutritional selection. Cookbooks with big colorful pictures make the search for a recipe more fun. Or sit down at the computer together and search through online recipes to find some. Help pick out some items they can make themselves and a few others you can do together.

Make sure the recipes focus on the nutritional needs of children. Most children need about 1,800 to 2,200 calories per day. Their meals each day should include six to nine servings of bread or cereal group, three or four servings of vegetables, two or three servings each of fruit, dairy, and protein (meat, poultry, fish, dry beans, eggs, or nuts). Keep this in mind when selecting recipes.

Pick some recipes that are suited to your child's abilities. If you are just getting started, you can try out some no-cook recipes to first. Once you've made a no-cook recipe out together, your kids might even be able to make it by themselves!

Young Coupon Masters

Your child can develop his or her fine motor skills by helping you clip coupons with a pair of kid-safe blunt-tip scissors. While you share in this activity, take an opportunity to introduce your child to the concept of coupons and explain how they work. Let them help you match the coupons to the items on your shopping list.

Shopping Sidekicks

Continue with the experience by having your child join you at the grocery store. You can make a game out of finding all the items on your list. Your kids don't have to move out on their own before learning how to pick out fresh produce and compare prices between brands. Resisting impulse buys is even harder for kids than it is for adults, so satisfy that compulsive urge by shopping on a day when your store gives out free samples. Teach them early that free is fun! Take your reusable shopping bags for a lesson in the environment and let the kids hold onto the recycling receipts when you return cans and bottles. Make sure to continue the lesson at home and have them help you put the groceries away.

Let's Get Cooking

Outfit your child with a few of his or her own tools. A child-sized apron is fun, and the dollar store often has inexpensive tools like measuring cups and wooden spoons. You can even set aside a little drawer or area of the kitchen where the kids can keep their equipment. Having their own space will teach them the value of organization, as well as give them a sense of ownership in the kitchen—not just Mom's domain, but a place where we cook together.

Teach your child the importance of starting out with a clean space before you start cooking. A clean kitchen is like a painter's blank canvas and less frustrating than trying to work around a mess. This is also a great opportunity to talk to kids about hygiene. Be sure everyone washes their hands and has their hair tied back. Dry your hands with a clean dishcloth or paper towels.

Careful preparation is key to a successful cooking session. Set out everything that you'll need, including all ingredients and tools. Explain how this helps you make sure that you have everything on hand and prevents any unnecessary trips to the store at the last minute.

Safety First

The kitchen is like a laboratory and should be treated with equal caution. Teach kids to avoid baggy clothing and dangly jewelry and to wear long hair up in a shower cap or a ponytail. You should handle major appliances yourself and supervise your child around electrical equipment and the hot stove. Be prepared to treat a few burns and cuts.

Things that may be obvious to us are not to kids. Be sure to demonstrate using potholders and standing back when opening the oven door. Show older kids proper knife technique so accidents don't happen.

Food safety is as important as kitchen safety. Keep cleaning products away from food. After you clean the kitchen for food prep, put chemicals away before you start getting out your ingredients.

Once you're done cooking, have children help you store leftovers, taking the opportunity to teach them about safe food handling to avoid spoilage and food-borne illnesses.

Following Directions

Reading the recipe is an opportunity for many lessons. Have your child read the recipe out loud and ask questions about the words they don't understand. Measuring ingredients is a lesson in math. Show how to choose the correct tools to measure different ingredients and how to use them accurately. Teach them that a recipe is like an instruction manual: you need to follow the directions to get the end product right.

Clean-Up Duty

Last but not least, make sure that kids help with washing dishes and putting things away. This should all be done before sitting down to enjoy the final product. This lesson will carry over to areas other than the kitchen: any project should be cleaned up before starting a new one, whether it's a batch of cookies or a jigsaw puzzle. Putting everything back the way it was before you began will make starting tomorrow's recipe that much easier.

General Tips for Cooking with Kids

Feed their interest. The best way to get a child interested in cooking is to start with stuff they already know they like. Chocolate chip cookies might make a better first recipe than, say, bulgur wheat with lima beans.

Set them up to feel accomplished. Be sure to praise your child often while cooking. If you have tips on what they can do better, don't frame them in a negative way. "You're doing it wrong" is just discouraging, whereas, "Think you're strong enough to knead this pizza dough like Mommy does it?" sounds more like a fun challenge.

Expect a mess. Kids are still developing their coordination and motor skills, so be prepared for some spills and messes. And besides, haven't we all dropped our fair share of eggs?

It's not about the perfect meal. The time you spend together with your children, instilling a love of cooking that will last a lifetime, is worth the occasional burnt casserole or rock-hard banana bread. If things don't go as planned, that's okay. Enjoy the time spent together.

Teach them to read labels. Food labels will teach your children more than the number of calories in a serving. Labels encourage portion control, help with math skills, and teach nutrition basics.

Kid-Friendly Cooking Ideas

Getting kids into the kitchen doesn't require a recipe, and in fact it may be better to start off without one. Here are some of my favorite things to make with my children.

NO OVEN REQUIRED

Banana pops. This is a great gluten-free treat. Peel a banana, dip it into melted chocolate, and freeze on a cookie sheet.

Yogurt shakes. Place yogurt, fruit, and milk or juice in a blender and whirl until till smooth.

No-cook kabobs. Skewer pieces of fruit or veggies onto bamboo skewer and serve with yogurt or dressing.

Ladybugs on a log. Fill a celery stick with raspberry-flavored cream cheese and top with dried cranberries.

PERSONAL PIZZAS

Grab some pizza dough and a variety of healthy toppings. Divide the dough into individually sized pieces—about the size of a tennis ball—and allow each child to pat out and top his or her own mini-pizza. This pizza doesn't have to be round or have evenly distributed toppings—let them get creative with shapes and designs. Buying premade pizza dough makes this a quick and easy meal for any night of the week. This makes a great birthday party!

TIPS FOR MAKING MUFFINS

Muffins are great to make with kids and provide endless opportunities for creativity. Below are a couple tips for making muffins:

* ❖ Don't overmix the batter or you'll end up with hard muffins. Small lumps are OK.

* ❖ Less butter and sugar makes a bread-like muffin, while more butter and sugar produces something closer to cake.

* ❖ Mix dry ingredients and wet ingredients separately and then blend together.

- ❀ Add fruit, nuts, or other add-ins after combining the wet and dry ingredients.

- ❀ Use a small ice cream scoop or big spoon to scoop the mix into the muffin tin.

- ❀ Spray the muffin tin with nonstick cooking spray or use paper liners for easy removal.

- ❀ The oven rack should be in the middle position for even heat distribution.

- ❀ Let muffins cool for a few minutes before turning them out of the pan onto a cooling rack.

- ❀ Muffins can be frozen for up to two months

SMOOTHIES

Smoothies are delicious, easy to make, full of nutrients, and essentially foolproof. Some smoothie tips:

- ❀ Try using frozen fruit in place of ice.

- ❀ Don't throw away those overripe bananas! They're perfect for smoothies. Toss browning bananas in the freezer and save them for the next time you whip up a smoothie.

- ❀ Preserve fresh berries for smoothies by freezing them on a cookie sheet. Once they're frozen, store them in resealable freezer bags.

- Add yogurt, milk, or even flax seeds to add some nutrition.
- Go light on sugar—the juice, fruit, and flavored yogurt already in your cool concoction go a long way toward sweetening the deal.

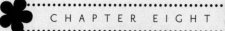

CHAPTER EIGHT

Budget Savvy Recipes

Most of my standard recipes that I use all the time
come from cooking in the kitchen with my family. It is
these recipes that really have shaped me as a person.

They've taught me many things, like how much money can be saved by cooking at home, but more meaningfully I've learned the importance of spending time with family. Included here are some of my favorite recipes from BudgetSavvyDiva.com, as well as brand new recipe that you will not find on the site. Remember to have fun when you cook!

INGREDIENT SUBSTITUTION FOR EGGS

Sometimes when you're baking, you don't have the egg you need on hand. This is an easy ingredient substitution for a similar result.

I egg = ¼ cup applesauce or ½ mashed banana

Pantry Basics You Can Make

- ❀ Frugal Marinara Sauce
- ❀ Homemade Cream of Vegetable Soup
- ❀ Hummus
- ❀ Pesto
- ❀ Mason Jar Balsamic Vinaigrette
- ❀ Red Wine Vinegar Salad Dressing
- ❀ Homemade Pam
- ❀ Homemade Baking Powder
- ❀ Homemade Bisquick
- ❀ Homemade Seasoned Salt
- ❀ Homemade Taco Seasoning
- ❀ Copy Cat Lipton Onion Soup Mix
- ❀ 1-Minute Homemade Ranch Seasoning Mix

Frugal Marinara Sauce

Makes 2 cups

3 to 4 tablespoons olive oil

1 large onion, chopped

5 garlic cloves, minced

1 (6-ounce) can tomato paste

1 tablespoon dried basil

2½ teaspoons dried oregano

½ teaspoon crushed red pepper flakes

1 (28-ounce) can whole tomatoes, undrained

⅓ to ½ cup dry red wine (optional)

½ teaspoon garlic powder

½ teaspoon onion powder

1 teaspoon sugar

1 teaspoon salt

freshly ground black pepper

IN A LARGE SAUCEPAN, HEAT THE OIL OVER MEDIUM HEAT. ADD THE ON-IONS AND GARLIC AND COOK FOR ABOUT 4 MINUTES.

ADD THE TOMATO PASTE AND STIR FOR 3 MINUTES.

ADD THE REST OF THE INGREDIENTS, REDUCE THE HEAT TO LOW, AND SIMMER UNCOVERED FOR 1½ HOURS, STIRRING OCCASIONALLY.

ENJOY WITH YOUR FAVORITE PASTA!

Homemade Cream of Vegetable Soup

Makes 1½ cups

Classic main ingredients will all taste great with this recipe. Try it with mushrooms.

¼ cup unsalted butter, divided
½ cup diced onion
½ cup main vegetable ingredient, your choice
2 garlic cloves, minced
¼ cup all-purpose flour
1 cup milk
¾ cup vegetable broth
pinch of salt
¼ teaspoon black pepper

MELT A SMALL AMOUNT OF THE BUTTER IN A LARGE SKILLET OVER MEDIUM HEAT. ADD THE ONIONS AND THE MAIN VEGETABLE INGREDIENT AND LET COOK FOR ABOUT 6 MINUTES UNTIL SOFTENED. ADD THE GARLIC AND COOK FOR 1 MINUTE. REMOVE THE VEGGIES FROM THE PAN AND SET ASIDE

ADD THE REMAINING BUTTER TO THE SKILLET AND MELT OVER MEDIUM HEAT. WHISK IN THE FLOUR AND COOK FOR 2 MINUTES, WHISKING CONSTANTLY. SLOWLY ADD THE MILK AND BROTH. ADD THE RESERVED COOKED VEGGIES AND BRING EVERYTHING TO A BOIL. REDUCE THE HEAT TO LOW AND SIMMER FOR 10 TO 15 MINUTES, UNTIL THE VEGETABLES ARE SOFT. STIR IN THE SALT AND PEPPER.

YOU CAN REFRIGERATE THE SOUP FOR UP TO 4 DAYS, OR YOU CAN FREEZE IT IN ZIPLOC BAGGIES.

Hummus

Serves 4 to 6

1 (15-ounce) can garbanzo beans
¼ cup tahini
3½ tablespoons lemon juice
2 garlic cloves, minced
½ teaspoon ground cumin
½ teaspoon salt
½ teaspoon pepper

DRAIN THE BEANS AND RESERVE THE LIQUID.

IN A BLENDER OR FOOD PROCESSOR, PUREE THE BEANS ALONG WITH ALL THE OTHER INGREDIENTS PLUS ¼ CUP OF THE LIQUID. BLEND UNTIL SMOOTH.

Pesto

Serves 4 to 6

2 cups fresh basil, packed
⅓ cup pine nuts
2 garlic cloves, minced
½ cup extra-virgin olive oil
½ cup grated Parmesan-Romano cheese blend
salt and freshly ground black pepper

PLACE THE PINE NUTS AND BASIL IN A FOOD PROCESSOR AND PULSE 3 TIMES. ADD THE GARLIC AND PULSE AGAIN. WITH THE PROCESSOR RUNNING, SLOWLY ADD THE OLIVE OIL UNTIL WELL BLENDED. ADD THE CHEESE, SEASON TO TASTE WITH SALT AND PEPPER, AND PULSE AGAIN TO COMBINE.

Mason Jar Balsamic Vinaigrette

Makes enough for 2 to 3 large salads

I love using a Mason jar for this supersimple dressing because it makes it so easy and fun to mix.

½ cup extra-virgin olive oil
I garlic clove, minced
pinch of salt
pinch of pepper
¼ cup balsamic vinegar

PLACE ALL THE INGREDIENTS IN A MASON JAR. MAKE SURE THE JAR IS SECURELY SEALED, AND SHAKE TO COMBINE.

Red Wine Vinegar Salad Dressing

Makes enough for 2 large salads

⅓ cup extra-virgin olive oil

⅓ cup red wine vinegar

1 tablespoon sugar

lemon zest

1 garlic clove, minced

½ teaspoon salt

¼ teaspoon freshly ground black pepper

PLACE ALL THE INGREDIENTS IN A MASON JAR OR ANOTHER JAR WITH A LID. SHAKE UNTIL ALL COMPONENTS ARE MIXED WELL. YOU CAN REFRIGERATE ANY EXTRA FOR UP TO 2 WEEKS.

Homemade Pam®

Makes ½ cup

¼ cup vegetable oil

¼ cup shortening (like Crisco)

¼ cup all-purpose flour

COMBINE ALL THE INGREDIENTS IN A MEDIUM BOWL. MIX WITH AN ELECTRIC BEATER ON MEDIUM SPEED UNTIL COMPLETELY MIXED. STORE IN AN AIRTIGHT CONTAINER IN THE CUPBOARD OR FRIDGE. BRUSH ON PANS OR MUFFIN TINS.

Homemade Baking Powder

Makes about 1 tablespoon

1 teaspoon baking soda
2 teaspoons cream of tartar
1 teaspoon cornstarch (optional)

MIX THE BAKING SODA AND CREAM OF TARTAR TOGETHER UNTIL WELL COMBINED. USE IMMEDIATELY. ADD THE CORNSTARCH TO BE ABLE TO STORE THE BAKING POWDER FOR UP TO 6 MONTHS. TO MAKE A LARGER SUPPLY TO KEEP ON HAND, INCREASE THE AMOUNTS OF EACH INGREDIENT PROPORTIONALLY.

Homemade Bisquick®

Makes 4½ cups

3¼ cups unsifted all-purpose flour
½ cup sugar
1 cup nonfat dry milk
½ cup cornstarch
1 tablespoon baking powder
1 teaspoon baking soda
1½ teaspoons salt

MIX ALL THE INGREDIENTS TOGETHER WELL. USE IT JUST LIKE YOU WOULD STORE-BOUGHT BISQUICK. STORE IN AN AIRTIGHT CONTAINER.

Homemade Seasoned Salt

Makes a little more than ⅓ cup

⅓ cup table salt

2 tablespoons sugar

2 teaspoons paprika

I teaspoon garlic powder

1½ teaspoons onion powder

½ teaspoon black pepper

½ teaspoon ground turmeric

pinch of cayenne pepper

¼ teaspoon crushed red pepper flakes (optional)

MIX ALL THE INGREDIENTS IN A SMALL BOWL.

Homemade Taco Seasoning

Makes about 1¼ ounces (equal to about 1 store-bought taco seasoning packet)

1 tablespoon chili powder

½ teaspoon garlic powder

¼ teaspoon onion powder

¼ teaspoon crushed red pepper flakes

¼ teaspoon cayenne pepper

½ teaspoon paprika

2 teaspoons ground cumin

1 teaspoon salt

1 teaspoon black pepper

MIX ALL INGREDIENTS TOGETHER IN A SMALL BOWL. USE 2 FULL TABLE-SPOONS OF TACO SEASONING FOR 1 POUND OF BEEF OR OTHER GROUND MEAT.

Copy Cat Lipton® Onion Soup Mix

Makes 2 ounces (equal to about 1 store-bought Lipton Onion Soup Mix packet)

¼ cup minced onion

3 tablespoons beef bouillon granules

⅛ teaspoon onion powder

⅛ teaspoon celery seed

⅛ teaspoon sugar

COMBINE ALL INGREDIENTS IN A SMALL BOWL.

TO MAKE CLASSIC ONION DIP: STIR 5 TABLESPOONS OF ONION SOUP MIX INTO I PINT OF SOUR CREAM.

1-Minute Homemade Ranch Seasoning Mix

2 tablespoons dried parsley

1 teaspoon dried dill

1 teaspoon garlic powder

1 teaspoon onion flakes

½ teaspoon dried basil

½ teaspoon black pepper

MIX ALL THE INGREDIENTS IN A BOWL.

STORE IN A ZIPLOC BAG OR MASON JAR.

TO MAKE RANCH DRESSING: WHISK 1 TABLESPOON OF THE HOMEMADE SEASONING MIX INTO ⅓ CUP MAYONNAISE OR ⅓ CUP NONFAT GREEK YOGURT. WHISK IN ¼ CUP MILK AND SEASON WITH SALT TO TASTE.

TO MAKE RANCH DIP: MIX 1 TABLESPOON OF THE HOMEMADE SEASONING MIX INTO 1½ CUPS SOUR CREAM. SEASON WITH SALT TO TASTE.

Main Dishes and Simple Sides

* Easy Banana Bread
* 7UP Biscuits
* Copycat Marie Callender's Cornbread
* Amazing Scrambled Eggs
* Red Pepper Egg-in-a-Hole
* Homemade Jalapeno Poppers
* Parmesan-Roasted Zucchini
* Ultimate Slow Cooker Mashed Potatoes
* Copy Cat Olive Garden Pasta Alfredo
* Slow Cooker Chicken Alfredo
* Slow Cooker Macaroni and Cheese
* Spinach and Artichoke Baked Pasta
* Simple Roasted Chicken
* Slow Cooker Whole Chicken
* Southwestern Egg Rolls with Avocado Ranch
* Southwestern Supreme Chicken Soup
* The Best Chicken Enchiladas
* Oven-Fried Chicken
* Slow Cooker Beef Barbecue
* Ham and Swiss Pockets

Easy Banana Bread

Serves 4 to 6

2 cups all-purpose flour

1 teaspoon baking soda

¼ teaspoon salt

½ cup unsalted butter, at room temperature

1 cup brown sugar, packed

2 large eggs, beaten

2 to 3 very overripe bananas, mashed

PREHEAT THE OVEN TO 350°F. GREASE A 9 X 5-INCH LOAF PAN. IN A MEDIUM BOWL, COMBINE THE FLOUR, BAKING SODA, AND SALT. IN A LARGE BOWL, MIX TOGETHER THE BUTTER, BROWN SUGAR, EGGS, AND BANANAS. SLOWLY ADD THE WET MIXTURE TO THE DRY MIXTURE AND STIR UNTIL WELL BLENDED. POUR THE BATTER INTO THE PREPARED LOAF PAN AND BAKE FOR 1 HOUR, UNTIL A TOOTHPICK INSERTED INTO THE BREAD COMES OUT CLEAN.

7UP® Biscuits

Makes 9

These biscuits are very addictive. Be prepared to make multiple batches.

½ cup sour cream

2 cups Homemade Bisquick (page 113)

½ cup lemon-lime soda

¼ cup melted unsalted butter or margarine

½ teaspoon garlic powder

PREHEAT THE OVEN TO 450°F. MIX THE SOUR CREAM AND BISQUICK TOGETHER, THEN ADD THE LEMON-LIME SODA. ON A FLAT SURFACE DUSTED WITH A SMALL AMOUNT OF BISQUICK, AND PAT THE DOUGH OUT TO ABOUT A 9-INCH SQUARE. CUT THE DOUGH INTO 9 EQUAL PIECES.

SPREAD HALF OF THE MELTED BUTTER IN A 9 × 9-INCH PAN. PLACE THE BISCUITS ON TOP OF THE MELTED BUTTER. DRIZZLE THE REST OF THE BUTTER ON TOP OF THE BISCUITS AND FINISH WITH A SPRINKLE OF GAR-LIC POWDER ON EACH BISCUIT. BAKE FOR ABOUT 15 MINUTES, UNTIL GOLDEN BROWN.

Copy Cat Marie Callender's® Cornbread

Serves 4 to 6

1½ cups Homemade Bisquick (page 113)

⅓ cup cornmeal

½ teaspoon baking powder

¾ cup sugar

2 eggs, beaten

1 cup milk

1 tablespoon unsalted butter, melted

PREHEAT OVEN TO 350°F AND BUTTER AN 8 X 8-INCH BAKING DISH. COMBINE THE BISQUICK, CORNMEAL, BAKING POWDER, AND SUGAR IN A LARGE BOWL. THEN ADD THE EGGS, MILK, AND MELTED BUTTER AND STIR TO COMBINE WELL. POUR THE BATTER INTO THE PREPARED BAKING DISH. BAKE FOR 30 TO 35 MINUTES, UNTIL A TOOTHPICK INSERTED INTO THE BREAD COMES OUT CLEAN.

Amazing Scrambled Eggs

Serves 2

4 eggs
1 tablespoon milk
pinch of salt
pinch of pepper
1 teaspoon unsalted butter
½ teaspoon Worcestershire sauce

WHISK THE EGGS, MILK, SALT, AND PEPPER TOGETHER IN A MEDIUM BOWL. MELT THE BUTTER IN A SKILLET OVER MEDIUM-LOW HEAT AND ADD THE EGGS. LET COOK FOR 1 MINUTE UNDISTURBED, THEN GENTLY STIR IN THE WORCESTERSHIRE SAUCE AND FINISH COOKING THE EGGS.

Red Pepper Egg-in-a-Hole

Serves 1

olive oil
I large red bell pepper, seeded and cut into ¾-inch rings
I egg
shredded cheddar cheese (optional)
salt and pepper

HEAT ENOUGH OIL TO LIGHTLY COVER A SKILLET OVER MEDIUM HEAT. PLACE A PEPPER RING ON THE SKILLET AND LET IT COOK FOR I MINUTE. BREAK EGG INTO THE RING. ALLOW IT TO COOK UNTIL THE WHITE IS MOSTLY SET. SEASON WITH A LITTLE SALT AND PEPPER. FLIP AND COOK FOR I MINUTE LONGER.

FOR A FUN VARIATION, WHISK THE EGG IN A SMALL BOWL WITH A PINCH EACH OF SALT AND PEPPER AND A LITTLE SHREDDED CHEESE. POUR THE MIXTURE INTO THE PEPPER RING IN THE SKILLET. ALLOW THE EGG TO ALMOST FULLY COOK, THEN FLIP AND COOK FOR I MINUTE LONGER.

Homemade Jalapeno Poppers

Makes 12

12 jalapeno peppers, sliced in half lengthwise, seeded
8 ounces cream cheese, at room temperature
2 eggs, beaten
2 tablespoons water
½ teaspoon salt
1 cup plain dry breadcrumbs
canola oil, for deep frying (optional)

LINE A BAKING SHEET WITH PARCHMENT PAPER. FILL EACH JALAPENO HALF WITH CREAM CHEESE AND PRESS THE HALVES BACK TOGETHER. IN A SMALL BOWL, COMBINE THE EGGS, WATER AND SALT. PLACE THE BREADCRUMBS IN A SECOND SMALL BOWL. DIP EACH JALAPENO INTO THE EGG MIXTURE, THEN THE BREADCRUMBS, THEN BACK INTO THE EGG MIXTURE, THEN BACK INTO THE BREADCRUMBS. ARRANGE ON THE PRE-PARED BAKING SHEET. FREEZE THE JALAPENOS FOR 2 HOURS.

TO FRY THE POPPERS, POUR ENOUGH OIL INTO A HEAVY POT TO COVER A JALAPENO AND HEAT THE OIL TO 350°F. FRY THE POPPERS FOR 1 TO 2 MINUTES, UNTIL GOLDEN BROWN, WORKING IN BATCHES IF NEEDED AND BEING CAREFUL NOT TO OVERCROWD THE PAN. DRAIN ON PAPER TOWELS.

TO BAKE THE POPPERS, PREHEAT THE OVEN TO 350°F. ARRANGE THE POPPERS ON A BAKING SHEET AND BAKE FOR ABOUT 15 MINUTES, UNTIL GOLDEN BROWN.

Parmesan-Roasted Zucchini

Serves 4

This supereasy side will be a hit with any meal. Extremely family-friendly. Gluten-free.

2 medium zucchini, quartered lengthwise

1 tablespoon olive oil

salt

black pepper

garlic powder

⅓ cup grated Parmesan cheese

PREHEAT THE OVEN TO 400°F AND LINE A BAKING SHEET WITH PARCHMENT PAPER.

LAY THE ZUCCHINI ON THE PREPARED SHEET, AND BRUSH EACH WITH OLIVE OIL AND SPRINKLE WITH SALT, PEPPER, AND GARLIC POWDER TO TASTE. TOP EVENLY WITH THE CHEESE. BAKE FOR ABOUT 15 MINUTES, UNTIL THE ZUCCHINI IS TENDER AND THE CHEESE IS BROWNED.

Ultimate Slow Cooker Mashed Potatoes

Serves 8 to 10

This dish is very easy to make and extremely yummy—you really can't go wrong with this one.

5 pounds russet potatoes

1½ cups chicken broth

¼ cup unsalted butter, cut into small cubes

1 garlic clove, minced

1¼ cups light sour cream

1 teaspoon salt

¼ teaspoon freshly ground black pepper

⅓ cup warm milk

2 ounces light cream cheese

PEEL AND CUBE THE POTATOES. I TRY TO GET 12 CUBES PER POTATO.

SET YOUR SLOW COOKER TO HIGH. PLACE THE POTATOES, CHICKEN BROTH, AND BUTTER IN THE SLOW COOKER AND COOK FOR 4½ HOURS.

ROUGHLY MASH THE COOKED POTATOES, THEN ADD THE REMAINING INGREDIENTS AND MASH TO COMBINE.

Copy Cat Olive Garden® Pasta Alfredo

Serves 6 to 8

1 pound pasta, any shape
½ cup (1 stick) unsalted butter
1 garlic clove, minced
2 cups (1 pint) heavy cream
2 tablespoons cream cheese
1 cup grated Parmesan cheese
salt and pepper

COOK THE PASTA ACCORDING TO THE PACKAGE DIRECTIONS. DRAIN IN A COLANDER AND COVER TO KEEP WARM.

MELT THE BUTTER IN A MEDIUM SAUCEPAN OVER MEDIUM HEAT. ADD THE GARLIC AND COOK, STIRRING, FOR 2 MINUTES. ADD THE CREAM AND CREAM CHEESE AND HEAT UNTIL MELTED AND BUBBLING, BUT NOT BOILING.

ADD THE PARMESAN CHEESE AND STIR UNTIL THE CHEESE MELTS. ADD SALT AND PEPPER TO TASTE; I USUALLY ADD ABOUT ½ TEASPOON PEPPER, BUT THAT'S JUST ME. TO SERVE, MIX A SMALL AMOUNT OF THE SAUCE WITH THE PASTA (A LITTLE SAUCE GOES A LONG WAY).

Slow Cooker Chicken Alfredo

Serves 4 to 6

olive oil

½ onion, chopped

1 cup roasted red pepper strips

1½ pounds boneless, skinless chicken breast, cut into bite-size pieces

1 garlic clove, minced

2 cups Alfredo sauce

4 cups frozen broccoli florets

¼ cup grated Parmesan cheese

1 tablespoon black pepper

Cooked pasta, to serve

HEAT ENOUGH OIL TO COAT A MEDIUM SKILLET OVER MEDIUM HEAT. ADD THE ONIONS AND RED PEPPERS AND SAUTÉ 5 TO 7 MINUTES, UNTIL THE ONIONS START TO BROWN. SET YOUR SLOW COOKER TO LOW. PLACE THE COOKED ONIONS AND PEPPERS IN THE SLOW COOKER ALONG WITH THE REMAINING INGREDIENTS AND STIR TO COMBINE.

COOK FOR ABOUT 4 HOURS OR UNTIL THE CHICKEN IS FULLY COOKED. SERVE WITH COOKED PASTA.

Slow Cooker Macaroni and Cheese

Serves 4 to 6

This mac 'n' cheese is heavenly.

2 cups elbow macaroni

¼ cup (½ stick) unsalted butter

2½ cups shredded sharp cheddar cheese

1 egg

½ cup sour cream

1 (10.75-ounce) can condensed cheddar cheese soup

1 cup 2% milk

½ teaspoon prepared yellow mustard

1 teaspoon black pepper

½ teaspoon onion powder

½ teaspoon garlic powder

pinch of nutmeg

pinch of cayenne pepper

BRING A LARGE POT OF SALTED WATER TO A BOIL. COOK THE PASTA FOR 6 MINUTES, THEN DRAIN IN A COLANDER AND SET ASIDE. NOTE THAT SOME PEOPLE FIND THAT COOKING THE PASTA FOR ONLY 3 MINUTES WORKS BETTER, BECAUSE THE PASTA RETAINS SOME OF ITS FIRMNESS AND IS MORE AL DENTE, ITALIAN FOR "TO THE TOOTH."

IN A MEDIUM SAUCEPAN OVER MEDIUM HEAT, MELT AND MIX THE BUTTER AND CHEESE TOGETHER. IN YOUR SLOW COOKER, MIX THE COOKED PASTA, MELTED BUTTER AND CHEESE, AND ALL THE REMAINING INGREDIENTS TOGETHER. COOK ON LOW FOR 2½ HOURS, STIRRING HOURLY. GARNISH WITH MORE CHEESE, IF DESIRED.

Spinach and Artichoke Baked Pasta

Serves 6

Comfort in a dish.

14 ounces orecchiette pasta, or other short pasta

1 tablespoon olive oil

1 cup chopped onion

3 garlic cloves, minced

1 cup sour cream

4 ounces cream cheese, at room temperature

¾ cup grated Parmesan cheese

1 teaspoon grated lemon zest, or to taste

1 teaspoon lemon juice, or to taste

10 ounces frozen spinach, thawed (make sure to squeeze out the excess moisture)

1 (13.5-ounce) can artichoke hearts, rinsed and chopped

½ teaspoon salt

1 teaspoon black pepper

1 cup shredded mozzarella cheese, divided

PREHEAT THE OVEN TO 425°F AND GREASE A 2½ TO 3-QUART CASSEROLE DISH.

COOK THE PASTA ACCORDING TO THE PACKAGE DIRECTIONS. RESERVE ¼ CUP OF THE PASTA WATER AND DRAIN THE REST. SET THE COOKED PASTA ASIDE.

HEAT THE OLIVE OIL IN A MEDIUM SKILLET, ADD THE ONIONS, AND COOK FOR 8 TO 10 MINUTES, UNTIL SOFTENED AND TRANSLUCENT. ADD THE GARLIC AND COOK, STIRRING, FOR 1 MINUTE.

IN A LARGE BOWL, MIX TOGETHER THE SOUR CREAM, CREAM CHEESE, PARMESAN CHEESE, LEMON ZEST AND JUICE, AND THE COOKED ON-IONS AND GARLIC. ADD THE COOKED PASTA AND MIX.

STIR IN THE SPINACH, ARTICHOKE HEARTS, THE RESERVED PASTA WATER, AND THE SALT, PEPPER, AND ½ CUP OF THE MOZZARELLA.

SPREAD THE MIXTURE IN THE PREPARED CASSEROLE DISH AND SPRINKLE THE REMAINING ½ CUP MOZZARELLA CHEESE ON TOP. BAKE FOR 10 TO 15 MINUTES, UNTIL GOLDEN BROWN ON TOP.

Simple Roasted Chicken

Serves 4 to 5

½ teaspoon salt

1 teaspoon black pepper

1 teaspoon onion powder

1 teaspoon garlic powder

1 (3-pound) whole chicken

1 lemon

½ cup unsalted butter

1 celery rib

5 garlic cloves

PREHEAT THE OVEN TO 350°F. IN A SMALL BOWL, MIX TOGETHER THE SALT, PEPPER, ONION POWDER, AND GARLIC POWDER. PLACE THE CHICKEN IN A ROASTING PAN AND SEASON INSIDE AND OUT WITH THE SEASONING MIXTURE. SQUEEZE THE LEMON JUICE OVER THE OUTSIDE OF THE CHICKEN AND PLACE THE LEMON RIND INSIDE THE CHICKEN CAVITY.

PLACE 3 TABLESPOONS OF THE BUTTER IN THE CHICKEN CAVITY, AND DOLLOP THE REMAINING BUTTER AROUND THE OUTSIDE OF THE CHICKEN.

CUT THE CELERY IN HALF AND PLACE INTO THE CHICKEN CAVITY. SLIDE THE WHOLE GARLIC CLOVES UNDER THE CHICKEN SKIN. BAKE UNCOVERED FOR 1 HOUR AND 15 MINUTES, UNTIL THE CHICKEN INTERNAL TEMPERATURE IS 180°F WHEN MEASURED WITH A MEAT THERMOMETER. LET THE CHICKEN REST FOR ABOUT 15 MINUTES, THEN SERVE.

Slow Cooker Whole Chicken

Serves 4 to 6

There's no liquid needed for this recipe; the chicken creates its own juices. The meat will be so tender that it will fall off the bones.

2 teaspoons salt

2 teaspoons paprika

½ teaspoon cayenne pepper

1 teaspoon onion powder

1 teaspoon dried thyme

1½ teaspoons black pepper

1 teaspoon garlic powder

1 (3-pound) roasting chicken

1 onion, chopped

IN A SMALL BOWL, MIX ALL THE SPICES TOGETHER.

PLACE THE CHOPPED ONIONS IN THE BOTTOM OF THE SLOW COOKER. RUB SPICE MIXTURE ON THE OUTSIDE OF THE CHICKEN, THEN ADD THE CHICKEN TO THE SLOW COOKER. COOK ON HIGH FOR 4 TO 5 HOURS, UNTIL THE CHICKEN'S INTERNAL TEMPERATURE IS 180°F WHEN TESTED WITH A MEAT THERMOMETER. ALLOW TO REST FOR 10 MINUTES BEFORE SERVING.

Southwestern Egg Rolls with Avocado Ranch Dipping Sauce

Serves 25

Egg Rolls:

50 egg roll or wonton wrappers

2 cups frozen corn kernels, thawed

1 (15-ounce) can black beans, rinsed and drained

1 (9-ounce) package frozen chopped spinach, thawed and
    squeezed dry with paper towels

2 cups shredded Mexican cheese

1 (4-ounce) can diced green chiles, drained

2 green onions, finely chopped

1 teaspoon ground cumin

½ teaspoon chili powder

½ teaspoon salt

½ teaspoon cayenne pepper

olive oil, for brushing

Dipping Sauce:

½ cup ranch salad dressing

½ medium ripe avocado, mashed

1 tablespoon minced fresh cilantro

1 teaspoon grated lime zest

FOR THE EGG ROLLS, PREHEAT THE OVEN TO 400°F AND LINE A RIMMED
BAKING SHEET WITH PARCHMENT PAPER. SET THE EGG ROLL OR WON-

TON WRAPPERS ASIDE. IN A LARGE BOWL, MIX ALL THE REMAINING EGG ROLL INGREDIENTS TOGETHER. ROLL THE EGG ROLLS IN THE WRAPPERS ACCORDING TO THE PACKAGE INSTRUCTIONS.

ONCE THEY ARE ALL WRAPPED, PLACE THE EGG ROLLS ON THE PREPARED BAKING SHEET. BRUSH A SMALL AMOUNT OF OLIVE OIL ONTO EACH ROLL AND BAKE FOR 15 MINUTES, UNTIL GOLDEN BROWN. ROTATE THE BAKING SHEET ONCE DURING BAKING.

WHILE THE EGG ROLLS ARE BAKING, STIR TOGETHER ALL THE INGREDIENTS FOR THE DIPPING SAUCE IN A MEDIUM BOWL. SERVE THE DIP WITH THE EGG ROLLS.

Southwestern Supreme Chicken Soup

Serves 4 to 6

I highly recommend garnishing your soup with diced avocado. Delicious!

½ cup chicken broth
2 cups milk
I teaspoon black pepper
I teaspoon ground cumin
½ teaspoon salt
I (15-ounce) can kidney beans
I (14.5-ounce) can Rotel Diced Tomatoes and Jalapenos
I (14.5-ounce) corn kernels, drained
½ cup finely chopped onion
½ green bell pepper, diced
grated zest and juice of I lime
I (16-ounce) can green enchilada sauce
I jalapeno, seeded and diced
3 boneless, skinless chicken breasts

Optional Garnishes:
shredded cheddar cheese
sour cream
diced avocado

MIX ALL THE INGREDIENTS EXCEPT THE CHICKEN TOGETHER IN YOUR SLOW COOKER. ADD THE CHICKEN (I NORMALLY CUT EACH CHICKEN BREAST IN HALF). COOK ON LOW FOR 6 TO 8 HOURS OR HIGH FOR 3 TO 4 HOURS.

AROUND HOUR 5 OR 2½, DEPENDING ON THE HEAT LEVEL, TAKE OUT THE CHICKEN AND SHRED IT. THIS STEP IS OPTIONAL BUT HIGHLY SUGGESTED. RETURN THE SHREDDED CHICKEN TO THE SLOW COOKER AND LET IT CONTINUE COOKING UNTIL DONE. GARNISH WITH SHREDDED CHEDDAR CHEESE, SOUR CREAM, AND DICED AVOCADO, IF DESIRED.

The Best Chicken Enchiladas

Serves 4 to 6

They're simply the best!

2 cups shredded cooked chicken, divided

2 cups shredded Monterey Jack cheese

1 garlic clove, minced

6 to 10 flour tortillas

3 tablespoons unsalted butter

2 tablespoons cornstarch

2 cups chicken broth

1 cup sour cream

1 jalapeno, seeded and finely chopped

1 teaspoon lime juice

1 teaspoon ground cumin

1 teaspoon onion powder

1 teaspoon garlic powder

½ teaspoon salt

½ teaspoon pepper

PREHEAT OVEN TO 350°F. GREASE A 9 × 13-INCH BAKING PAN.

IN A MEDIUM BOWL MIX THE CHICKEN, 1 CUP OF THE CHEESE, AND THE GARLIC. ROLL THE MIXTURE INTO THE TORTILLAS AND PLACE IN THE PAN.

IN A SAUCEPAN, MELT THE BUTTER. STIR IN THE CORNSTARCH AND COOK FOR 1 MINUTE. ADD THE BROTH AND WHISK UNTIL SMOOTH. CONTINUE COOKING UNTIL IT BUBBLES AND BECOMES THICK. STIR IN THE SOUR

CREAM, JALAPENO, LIME JUICE, CUMIN, ONION POWDER, GARLIC POW-
DER, SALT, AND PEPPER. DO NOT LET IT BOIL.

POUR THE MIXTURE OVER THE ENCHILADAS AND TOP WITH THE RE-
MAINING I CUP CHEESE. BAKE FOR 25 MINUTES, UNTIL THE CHEESE HAS
BROWNED.

Oven-Fried Chicken

Serves 4 to 6

½ cup all-purpose flour

1½ tablespoons salt

½ teaspoons black pepper

½ teaspoons paprika

½ teaspoons garlic powder

½ teaspoons onion powder

1 (3-pound) whole chicken, cut into pieces

PREHEAT THE OVEN TO 450°F.

PLACE ALL THE INGREDIENTS EXCEPT THE CHICKEN IN A LARGE ZIPLOC BAG AND SHAKE TO COMBINE.

WASH THE CHICKEN PIECES AND PAT DRY TO MAKE SURE THERE IS NO EXCESS WATER. ONE PIECE AT A TIME, PLACE THE CHICKEN IN THE BAG WITH THE SPICES, SEAL THE BAG, AND SHAKE TO COAT. ARRANGE THE CHICKEN SKIN-SIDE DOWN ON A BAKING SHEET. BAKE FOR ABOUT 20 MINUTES, THEN FLIP OVER AND BAKE UNTIL GOLDEN BROWN, 10 TO 15 MINUTES LONGER.

Ham and Swiss Pockets

Serves 4 to 6

1 package refrigerated crescent rolls (8 rolls)
1½ cups shredded Swiss cheese
1½ cups chopped cooked ham

PREHEAT THE OVEN TO 375°F. UNROLL THE CRESCENT ROLLS INTO 4 PORTIONS. PINCH ANY REMAINING PERFORATIONS TO SEAL THEM. IN A MEDIUM BOWL, MIX THE CHEESE AND HAM TOGETHER. DIVIDE THE MIXTURE EVENLY AMONG THE ROLLS AND PLACE IN THE CENTERS. FOLD EACH ROLL IN HALF SO IT CREATES A POCKET, AND SEAL ALL THE OPEN EDGES. BAKE FOR 12 TO 15 MINUTES, UNTIL GOLDEN BROWN . LET COOL BEFORE SERVING.

Slow Cooker Beef Barbecue

Serves 4 to 6

olive oil, for cooking

3 pounds ground beef

1 large onion, chopped

3 garlic cloves, minced

3 celery ribs, chopped

1 teaspoon salt

1½ teaspoons black pepper

½ teaspoon crushed red pepper flakes

1 tablespoon cider vinegar

½ cup brown sugar, packed

3 tablespoons prepared yellow mustard

2½ cups ketchup

IN A SKILLET, HEAT THE OIL OVER MEDIUM HEAT AND BROWN THE MEAT. DRAIN OFF ANY EXCESS GREASE. ADD THE COOKED MEAT TO YOUR SLOW COOKER ALONG WITH ALL THE OTHER INGREDIENTS AND MIX. COOK ON LOW FOR 6 TO 8 HOURS, UNTIL HEATED THROUGH.

Drinks and Desserts

- 🍀 Homemade Sweet Tea
- 🍀 Homemade Gatorade
- 🍀 Apple Pie Cake
- 🍀 Homemade Chocolate Cake Mix
- 🍀 Cheesecake-Stuffed Strawberries with Chocolate Drizzle

Homemade Sweet Tea

Serves 4 to 6

pinch of baking soda
2 cups boiling water
6 black tea bags
¾ cup sugar
6 cups cool water

SPRINKLE THE BAKING SODA INTO A 64-OUNCE HEATPROOF GLASS PITCHER. POUR IN THE BOILING WATER AND ADD TEA BAGS. COVER AND ALLOW TO STEEP FOR 15 MINUTES.

REMOVE THE TEA BAGS AND DISCARD. STIR IN THE SUGAR UNTIL DISSOLVED. POUR IN THE COOL WATER, THEN REFRIGERATE UNTIL COLD.

Homemade Gatorade®

Serves 4 to 6

2 quarts (8 cups) water
1 teaspoon baking soda
1½ teaspoons salt
7 tablespoons sugar
1 (.16-ounce) packet Kool-Aid

MIX ALL THE INGREDIENTS TOGETHER IN A LARGE PITCHER. CHILL AND SERVE.

Apple Pie Cake

Serves 4 to 6

1 (16-ounce) box angel food cake mix
1 (21-ounce) can apple pie filling

FOLLOW THE BAKING INSTRUCTIONS ON THE CAKE BOX, BUT DON'T ADD ANY OF THE WET INGREDIENTS CALLED FOR IN THE RECIPE ON THE BOX. INSTEAD, MIX THE APPLE PIE FILLING INTO THE BATTER. BAKE ACCORDING TO THE BOX INSTRUCTIONS.

Homemade Chocolate Cake Mix

Serves 4 to 6

1 (9 x 13-inch) cake
2⅓ cups all-purpose flour
⅓ cup nonfat dry milk
1 tablespoon baking powder
¾ teaspoon salt
1½ cups sugar
½ cup plus 1 tablespoon shortening
¼ cup unsweetened cocoa powder

MIX ALL THE INGREDIENTS TOGETHER IN A LARGE AIRTIGHT CONTAINER AND KEEP IN A DRY PLACE. THE MIX WILL LAST FOR UP TO 6 MONTHS.

TO MAKE CAKE FROM THE MIX, PREHEAT THE OVEN TO 350°F AND GREASE A 9 X 13-INCH BAKING PAN. ADD 1⅓ CUPS WATER, ½ CUP VEGETABLE OIL, AND 3 EGGS. MIX UNTIL WELL COMBINED. BAKE FOR 30 TO 40 MINUTES, UNTIL TOOTHPICK INSERTED INTO THE CENTER COMES OUT CLEAN.

Cheesecake-Stuffed Strawberries with Chocolate Drizzle

Makes 10

Simple, delicious, and ready to enjoy in ten minutes. Can be made ahead of time. Gluten-free.

10 strawberries
4 ounces cream cheese, at room temperature (I use low-fat)
¼ cup powdered sugar
splash vanilla extract
⅓ cup semisweet chocolate chips

CUT THE TOPS OFF THE STRAWBERRIES AND WITH A SHARP KNIFE CUT AN X ON THE BOTTOM OF EACH ONE. DO NOT CUT ALL THE WAY THROUGH THE STRAWBERRY.

IN A MEDIUM BOWL, MIX THE CREAM CHEESE, POWDERED SUGAR, AND VANILLA. TRANSFER THE MIXTURE INTO A PASTRY BAG OR A PLASTIC BAG WITH THE TIP CUT OFF AND PIPE THE FILLING INTO EACH STRAWBERRY.

MELT THE CHOCOLATE CHIPS IN THE MICROWAVE, MAKING SURE NOT TO BURN THE CHOCOLATE. DRIZZLE THE CHOCOLATE ON TOP OF THE STRAWBERRIES.

CHAPTER NINE

Leftovers

Using leftovers creatively is one of the best ways
to save money in the kitchen. Did you know that
American households throw away
$600 worth of food every year?

We've all been guilty of it at one time or another. That asparagus looked great at the grocery store a month ago, but now it looks like a science experiment gone wrong in the back of the fridge. Or you ordered too much at a restaurant, only to have the leftovers morph into an inedible mess that you wouldn't even feed to your dog.

I try to have leftovers for lunch at least once a week. If you know a certain dinner item will get carted to the office for lunch tomorrow, portion and pack it right away so you don't have to worry about it in the morning.

But the possibilities for leftovers go beyond tomorrow's cubicle fare. Here are some simple ways to use up leftover food and stretch your dining dollars. Whether it's the remains of a home-cooked dinner or something you bring home in a doggie bag, leftovers can stretch into new and delicious meals. Some of my favorite meals came from leftovers. It just takes a little creativity!

Restaurant Leftovers

The portions served in U.S. restaurants are famous for being more than most people can—or should—eat. This phenomenon has been cited as one of the reasons for our current obesity epidemic. Although it can be hard to regulate your food intake when faced with a huge plate, thinking ahead to how you can turn those leftovers into a healthy second meal might help you slow down. I'm not talking about just reheating them (though there's nothing wrong with that), but turning the contents of your doggie bag into the basis for an entirely different meal. You may stop picking at your plate when you realize that the remains of Saturday night's fajitas can easily become Sunday morning's brunch.

Home-Cooked Leftovers

Don't let the leftovers from your homemade dinner take up space in the fridge until they go bad. You worked hard to make that food and it shouldn't go to waste. Sure, you can warm them up for lunch the next day, but you can also get creative and turn those leftovers from dinner tonight into another dinner tomorrow night. Think how much you could save! Stash those leftovers in the fridge and check your pantry to see what's on hand to make a great second meal.

Using Leftovers

If you're taking a doggie bag home from the restaurant, plan to refrigerate your leftovers within two hours to avoid food spoilage. If the temperature is above 90°F, make that one hour. When reheating in the microwave, add water to avoid drying out your food (especially rice), unless it's in a sauce, and be sure to use a microwave-safe container (avoid reheating in Styrofoam). Stir partway through the cooking time to avoid spot heating.

There are many ways you can incorporate leftovers into another meal. Below are a few of my favorites:

Make soup. Use various scraps of meat and veggies from your leftovers to make a soup—just add stock and maybe some fresh herbs. My Homemade Cream of Vegetable Soup (page 109) is perfect for this!

Fill up tacos. Leftover hamburgers and beef can be transformed into taco filling. Homemade Taco Seasoning (page 115) is perfect for spicing up taco night.

Make a sandwich. This is so simple: leftover meat between two pieces of bread. Don't forget to use up those veggies as well.

The Everything Salad. One of my favorites. Take a large bowl and start tossing in your leftover grilled veggies, sliced steak, crumbled cheese, whatever you've got. Toss with dressing (like my Mason Jar Balsamic Vinaigrette, page 111) and you are ready to eat!

Bread crumbs and croutons. Cut leftover bread into bite-size pieces, season with some Italian seasoning, drizzle with a little butter, and bake at 400°F for 10 minutes or until golden brown. To make breadcrumbs, place the croutons in a resealable plastic bag and use a rolling pin to smash them to fine crumbs. Try them in the Homemade Jalapeno Poppers recipe on page 124.

Dry it. Almost any food can be dried and preserved. Use a food dehydrator to make your own fruit chips and jerkies. These make a perfect snack for kids.

Bake it. Who doesn't love zucchini bread?! Leftover zucchini, bananas, and strawberries (to name just a few) can be incorporated into breads, cakes, and cobblers.

Melt it. Leftover cheese is a perfect addition to a homemade mac and cheese.

Throw it in the slow cooker. My favorite. Throw leftover chicken, steak, or other meat in the slow cooker with some type of liquid (even soda), and you're done! Serve with rice or pasta.

Need more inspiration? Here are some ideas for the leftovers we commonly find lurking in our fridge. Remember that leftovers have already been seasoned, so be careful not to over-salt when cooking with them.

Chicken

❀ Make chicken salad.

❀ Add it to a green salad.

❀ Put it in soup (like the Southwestern Supreme Chicken Soup, page 136).

❀ Shred it up for The Best Chicken Enchiladas (page 138).

Steak

✤ Slice it up and sauté with veggies, soy sauce, ginger, and a little sesame oil for a great stir-fry.

✤ Add it to a green salad.

✤ Use it to make fajitas.

✤ Wrap sliced steak in a low-carb tortilla with lettuce and other fixings (or just use lettuce as the wrapper).

✤ Grill it in a skillet with mushrooms, sliced yellow onions, and green onions. Add cheese and you've got a cheese steak. You can eat on a soft white roll, but it's just as good with nothing but a fork.

Fish

✤ It's not just for tuna anymore: any fish can be mixed with mayonnaise and made into a salad. Salmon salad is nice with sweet pickle relish in it.

✤ Add it to a green salad.

✤ Salmon is great in egg dishes like quiche.

✤ Mix coconut milk and Asian curry paste (such as Thai) to use as a sauce for fish curry.

Hamburger

❉ Mix hamburger with chopped vegetables and use to stuff vegetables or serve over rice.

❉ Crumble and use it in pasta sauce.

❉ Combine with veggies and spices to make a hash. I love to mix in rice and a little Worcestershire sauce.

Chili

❉ Make a chili cheese omelet.

❉ Use it to top fries or a baked potato.

❉ Top a hamburger or hot dog for a chili burger or chili dog.

❉ Serve over spaghetti squash, low-carb pasta, or even rice!

❉ Turn into a whole new chili by adding different spices, vegetables, or beans.

Veggies

❉ Make them the main ingredient in a soup, or use them to bulk up a stew.

❉ Use them in a casseroles for breakfast or dinner.

❉ Mix them into scrambled eggs with some cheese.

Chinese Food

✿ Turn leftover rice into fried rice. Chop up any meat and veggies and add them in (keeping in mind that any sauces will influence the flavor).

✿ Serve with noodles.

Mexican Food

✿ Heat it up and mix with rice.

✿ Wrap it in leftover in tortillas.

Remember to be creative! Think pasta, soup, casseroles, eggs, and sandwiches. There are endless possibilities.

Appendix

Sources

Allrecipes.com. "Healthy Snacks for Kids: Smoothies," http://allrecipes.com/howto/healthy-snacks-for-kids-smoothies.

Barns, Liza and Nicole Nichols. "The Benefits of Growing Your Own Food," http://www.sparkpeople.com/resource/nutrition_articles.asp?id=1275.

Danger, Kimberley. *Instant Bargains: 600+ Ways to Shrink Your Grocery Bills and Eat Well for Less.* Naperville, IL: Sourcebooks, 2010.

The Daring Kitchen. "Quick Breads/Muffins & Popovers!" February 2012, http://thedaringkitchen.com/recipe/quick-breadsmuffins-popovers.

Dolson, Laura. "Using Up Leftovers," February 11, 2009, http://lowcarbdiets.about.com/od/cooking/a/doggiebagdining.htm.

Fitzpatrick, Diane Laney. "Easy, Delicious Fruit Smoothies," June 13, 2008, http://suite101.com/article/easy-delicious-fruit-smoothies-a56997.

Lu, Xin. "Simple Strategies for Using Your Leftover Food," August 10, 2010, http://www.wisebread.com/simple-strategies-for-using-your-leftover-food.

Conversions

I pound all-purpose flour = 3½ cups = 437 grams

I pound granulated sugar = 2¼ cups = 450 grams

I stick butter = ¼ pound = 110 grams

MEASURE	EQUIVALENT	METRIC
I teaspoon	--	5.0 milliliters
I tablespoon	3 teaspoons	14.8 milliliters
I cup	16 tablespoons	236.8 milliliters
I pint	2 cups	473.6 milliliters
I quart	4 cups	947.2 milliliters
I liter	4 cups + 3½ tablespoons	1000 milliliters
I ounce (dry)	2 tablespoons	28.35 grams
I fluid ounce	2 tablespoons	30 milliliters
I pound	16 ounces	453.49 grams
2.21 pounds	35.3 ounces	I kilogram
325°F/350°F/375°F	--	165°C/177°C/190°C

Acknowledgments

I am humbled that I was approached to write this book and know that I never would have received this great opportunity without the support and love of some very special people. I would not be where I am today without my "rock," the *Budget Savvy Diva* readers. They keep me going each and every single day.

I want to thank my grandfather, Edward Jagla, for instilling in me the philosophy of saving money and working hard in school. Also to my parents, John and Elizabeth, thank you for being there for me and letting me take over the kitchen every night as a child. Of course, my husband has been with me since day one of this crazy adventure. Thank you Eric for listening to me, being so supportive, and eating all my recipes, even when they were flops. I cannot forget Watson, who sat with me at all hours of the night while I wrote this book. I also would like to thank Ulysses Press, who gave me a chance to write this book and spread my message. Finally, I cannot forget my blogging assistants—without them I would never get any sleep.

About the Author

SARA LUNDBERG was raised in Los Angeles, California, and is a USC graduate whose passion for saving money extends from early childhood. Her website, www.BudgetSavvyDiva.com, aims to help people spend less and still have fun. Her dedication to consumer awareness of deals, bargains, and coupon fraud, in addition to her 24/7 updates, has caught the attention of over 1 million readers each month. Sara is also a talented and experienced cook, whose fish taco recipe made her a semifinalist in a national food competition. Her easy, low-cost recipes are just another reason people love the Budget Savvy Diva. She lives in Portland, Oregon.